Few and Far

Stolen Asset Recovery (StAR) Series

StAR—the Stolen Asset Recovery Initiative—is a partnership between the World Bank Group and the United Nations Office on Drugs and Crime (UNODC) that supports international efforts to end safe havens for corrupt funds. StAR works with developing countries and financial centers to prevent the laundering of the proceeds of corruption and to facilitate more systematic and timely return of stolen assets.

The Stolen Asset Recovery (StAR) Series supports the efforts of StAR and UNODC by providing practitioners with knowledge and policy tools that consolidate international good practice and wide-ranging practical experience on cutting edge issues related to anticorruption and asset recovery efforts. For more information, visit www.worldbank.org/star.

Titles in the Stolen Asset Recovery (StAR) Series

Stolen Asset Recovery: A Good Practices Guide for Non-Conviction Based Asset Forfeiture (2009) by Theodore S. Greenberg, Linda M. Samuel, Wingate Grant, and Larissa Gray

Politically Exposed Persons: Preventive Measures for the Banking Sector (2010) by Theodore S. Greenberg, Larissa Gray, Delphine Schantz, Carolin Gardner, and Michael Latham

Asset Recovery Handbook: A Guide for Practitioners (2011) by Jean-Pierre Brun, Larissa Gray, Clive Scott, and Kevin Stephenson

Barriers to Asset Recovery: An Analysis of the Key Barriers and Recommendations for Action (2011) by Kevin Stephenson, Larissa Gray, and Ric Power

The Puppet Masters: How the Corrupt Use Legal Structures to Hide Stolen Assets and What to Do About It (2011) by Emile van der Does de Willebois, J.C. Sharman, Robert Harrison, Ji Won Park, and Emily Halter

Public Office, Private Interests: Accountability through Income and Asset Disclosure (2012)

On the Take: Criminalizing Illicit Enrichment to Fight Corruption (2012) by Lindy Muzila, Michelle Morales, Marianne Mathias, and Tammar Berger

Left out of the Bargain: Settlements in Foreign Bribery Cases and Implications for Asset Recovery (2014) by Jacinta Anyango Oduor, Francisca M. U. Fernando, Agustin Flah, Dorothee Gottwald, Jeanne M. Hauch, Marianne Mathias, Ji Won Park, and Oliver Stolpe.

All books in the Stolen Asset Recovery (StAR) Series are available for free at https://openknowledge.worldbank.org/handle/10986/2172

Few and Far

The Hard Facts on Stolen Asset Recovery

Larissa Gray
Kjetil Hansen
Pranvera Recica-Kirkbride
Linnea Mills

StAR Stolen Asset Recovery Initiative

The World Bank • UNODC

OECD

ISBN: 978-1-4648-0274-4
e-ISBN: 978-1-4648-0275-1
DOI: 10.1596/978-1-4648-0274-4

Cover: Debra Naylor, Naylor Design, Inc.

Library of Congress Cataloging-in-Publication Data has been applied for

Contents

Boxes

Figures

Tables

StAR and OECD

StAR

The Stolen Asset Recovery Initiative is a partnership between the World Bank Group and the United Nations Office on Drugs and Crime that supports international efforts to end safe havens for corrupt funds. StAR works with developing countries and financial centers to prevent the laundering of the proceeds of corruption and to facilitate more systematic and timely return of stolen assets.

For more information, visit *www.worldbank.org/star*.

OECD DEVELOPMENT ASSISTANCE COMMITTEE

To achieve its aims, the OECD has set up a number of specialised committees. One of these is the Development Assistance Committee (DAC), whose mandate is to promote development co-operation and other policies so as to contribute to sustainable development—including pro-poor economic growth, poverty reduction and the improvement of living standards in developing countries—and to a future in which no country will depend on aid. To this end, the DAC has grouped the world's main donors, defining and monitoring global standards in key areas of development.

The members of the DAC are Australia, Austria, Belgium, Canada, the Czech Republic, Denmark, the European Union, Finland, France, Germany, Greece, Iceland, Ireland, Italy, Japan, Korea, Luxembourg, the Netherlands, New Zealand, Norway, Poland, Portugal, the Slovak Republic, Slovenia, Spain, Sweden, Switzerland, the United Kingdom and the United States.

The DAC issues guidelines and reference documents in the DAC Guidelines and Reference Series to inform and assist members in the conduct of their development co-operation programmes.

For more information, visit *www.oecd.org/dac*

Acknowledgments

This publication was a joint effort of the World Bank/UNODC Stolen Asset Recovery (StAR) Initiative and the Organisation for Economic Co-operation and Development (OECD). It was written by Larissa Gray (Task Team Leader, Senior Financial Sector Specialist, StAR Initiative), Kjetil Hansen (Lead Governance Advisor, OECD), Pranvera Recica-Kirkbride (Consultant, StAR Initiative), and Linnea Mills (Consultant, OECD).

The team is especially grateful to Jean Pesme (Coordinator, StAR Initiative), Alan Whaites (Team Lead, Governance OECD/DAC), and Phil Mason (Chair of the OECD/DAC Anti-Corruption Task Team) for their ongoing support and guidance on this project.

The team benefited from many insightful comments during the peer review process, which was chaired by Jean Pesme. The peer reviewers were Rita Adam (Department of Foreign Affairs, Switzerland); Joe Barker (Home Office, United Kingdom); Frank Fariello (Legal Vice Presidency, World Bank); Robert Leventhal (United States Department of State); Astrid Manroth (Operations Policy and Country Services, World Bank); Phil Mason (Department for International Development, United Kingdom); Ji Won Park (StAR Initiative); Tim Steele (United Nations Office on Drugs and Crime); Oliver Stolpe (StAR Initiative); and Teresa Turner-Jones (United States Department of Justice). The team also benefited from the input of Jeanne Hauch (StAR Initiative) and Alice Ahn (United States Department of State).

We would also like to thank Patricia Katayama, Mayya Revzina, and Rick Ludwick for their support and guidance in the publications process.

A special thanks to Eli Bielasiak (StAR Initiative), Maria Orellano (World Bank), and Louis Scott (OECD) for their support in the administration of the project, and to Alessandra Fontana (OECD) for her contributions during the publication process.

Abbreviations

AFAR	Arab Forum on Asset Recovery
DFID	U.K. Department for International Development
FATF	Financial Action Task Force
FIU	Financial intelligence unit
MLA	Mutual legal assistance
NCB	Non-conviction based
OECD	Organisation for Economic Co-operation and Development
PEP	Politically exposed person
SFO	U.K. Serious Fraud Office
StAR	Stolen Asset Recovery Initiative
UNCAC	United Nations Convention against Corruption.

All monetary values have been converted to United States dollars using the official exchange rate averages published by the World Bank (http://data.worldbank .org/indicator/PA.NUS.FCRF). For conversion of the euro, the yearly average exchange rates published by the U.S. Internal Revenue Services were used (http:// www.irs.gov/Individuals/International-Taxpayers/Yearly-Average-Currency -Exchange-Rates).

Executive Summary

Corruption besieges countries around the world, with the most devastating impact on developing and transition countries. It slows economic growth and development, diverting resources that could be used for development. It negatively affects the quality and accessibility of public services and infrastructure, erodes public confidence in government, reduces private sector development, and weakens the rule of law.

The seizure and recovery of the proceeds of corruption—asset recovery—is a powerful tool to combat corruption. Development agencies and other stakeholders committed to improving development effectiveness should be interested in using asset recovery as a means to combat corruption.

In the first place, the return of the proceeds of corrupt activities can have an important development impact when returns are used for development purposes: Recent examples have resulted in improvements in the health and education sectors and in the reintegration of displaced persons. Asset recovery also helps to deter corruption by showing that corrupt officials will be deprived of their illicit gains. Finally, additional benefits accrue in terms of improved international cooperation and enhanced capacity of law enforcement and financial management officials.

Development agencies have made international commitments to fight corruption and recover the proceeds of corruption at the *Third High-Level Forum on Aid Effectiveness: Accra Agenda for Actions*, held in Accra (2008); and *Fourth High-Level Forum on Aid Effectiveness: Partnership for Effective Development Co-operation,* in Busan (2011).

The implementation of those Accra and Busan commitments is the focus of this report by the Stolen Asset Recovery Initiative (StAR) and the Organisation for Economic Co-operation and Development (OECD) Development Assistance Committee. How have those commitments been translated into domestic policies, law, or institutional changes? What results have been achieved? How has asset recovery been incorporated into development policies and programs? The report focuses on the progress of 34 OECD members toward meeting those commitments between 2010 and June 2012. It is the second of its kind, following the StAR and OECD report of 2011, which measured progress from 2006 to 2009. Outlined below are the key findings and recommendations.

Key Findings

- *Since the first StAR/OECD report, the total assets frozen have increased*. A total of US$1.398 billion was frozen between 2010 and 2012. This activity over a

2.5 year period is already greater than that during the 4-year period covered by the first StAR/OECD report.

- **The legal avenues and powers used most successfully to freeze and return assets were not the "traditional" ones.** Administrative actions were introduced to freeze assets rapidly, and more jurisdictions proactively initiated their own investigations, rather than waiting for a request from the jurisdiction of the corrupt official. Non-conviction based confiscation, court-ordered reparations and restitution, and settlement agreements were used to return more assets than was criminal confiscation—commonly thought to be the main legal avenue for asset recovery.

- **OECD members are returning more assets to developing countries.** The first StAR/OECD report found that most returns were to other developed countries, whereas recent data show significant returns to developing countries.

- **Building the capacity of practitioners in developing countries can support asset recovery efforts.** Such initiatives have helped to prioritize and initiate cases, build trust with foreign counterparts, and eventually generate evidence (or a court order) to support asset recovery.

- **Countries with established asset recovery policies and solid legal and institutional frameworks continue to achieve success in returning the proceeds of corruption.** Only three OECD members—Switzerland, the United States, and the United Kingdom—have repatriated corruption proceeds in both reporting periods. All three countries have high-level policies, a wide range of asset recovery tools available, and dedicated teams working on asset recovery cases. Where barriers are encountered, new laws or creative solutions are sought to overcome them.

- **For the majority of OECD members, there is a disconnect between high-level international commitments and practice at the country level.** Fourteen of the 34 OECD members did not respond to the StAR survey at all,[1] and of those that responded, most reported very little progress. Experience has demonstrated that where such lack of interest and low-priority treatment extend to ineffective laws or institutions, criminals will exploit those vulnerabilities to launder corruption proceeds.

- **The data on asset recovery cases continue to be scarce.** Little progress was made in overcoming the obstacles identified in the first StAR/OECD report.

- **Few and Far: Ultimately, a huge gap remains between the results achieved and the billions of dollars that are estimated stolen from developing countries.** Only US$147.2 million was returned by OECD members between 2010 and June 2012, and US$276.3 million between 2006 and 2009, a fraction of the $20–40 billion estimated to have been stolen each year.

Main Recommendations

Success in stolen asset recovery requires coordinated action by all stakeholders in both requested and requesting jurisdictions, including those responsible for setting policies, law enforcement and justice officials, banks, private companies and their intermediaries

---

1. Responses were not received from Austria, Chile, Czech Republic, Estonia, Finland, Greece, Hungary, Iceland, Ireland, Korea, Mexico, Poland, Slovenia, and Turkey.

(e.g., lawyers), development cooperation actors, civil society, and the media. The following are the main recommendations for OECD DAC members and other development partners, based on survey results and independent research. Additional recommendations appear throughout the report and are intended to complement and expand on the priority ones. Although they may not be specific action areas for development agencies, all are activities that development agencies can foster and encourage to implement their Accra and Busan commitments.

1. ***Obtain a high-level commitment to asset recovery.*** Both developed and developing countries need to adopt and implement comprehensive strategic policies to combat corruption and recover assets. For their part, development agencies need to establish asset recovery as a priority in their strategic planning.

2. ***Provide the necessary resources.*** Adequate funding is needed to support asset recovery, including funding for investigations, prosecutions, international cooperation, training of domestic and foreign practitioners, policy development work, and institutions. Development agencies can allocate development funds to support these programs, both domestically and in foreign jurisdictions.

3. ***Ensure that a wide range of asset recovery tools are available and used.*** Both developed and developing countries need to ensure that they have a broad range of mechanisms in place, such as the abilities to rapidly freeze assets, to confiscate in the absence of a conviction, to return assets as part of a settlement agreement, and to reverse or shift the burden of proof.

4. ***Be proactive, not reactive.*** OECD members need to ensure that they are able to proactively identify and freeze the assets of allegedly corrupt officials and establish incentives for domestic practitioners to initiate cases. Such domestic actions should be followed by international cooperation with the relevant foreign jurisdiction, including spontaneous disclosures and actions to build capacity and trust. Developing countries need to be initiating their own investigations and communicating and cooperating with foreign counterparts.

5. ***Build capacity in developing countries.*** Asset recovery requires effective investigations in both the requested and requesting countries, and many developing countries may need technical assistance to take such action. Development agencies can support the training and mentoring of developing country practitioners, especially given that capacity development is a priority of the Accra Agenda and is key to achieving development results.

6. ***Collect statistics to measure results, and make them publicly available.*** Statistics on law enforcement activities are essential for showing that countries are fulfilling their high-level commitments; they also help to guide domestic policy development, resource allocation, and strategic planning. Making progress publicly available highlights results and also supports transparency and accountability, principles which the Busan Partnership and Paris Declaration have highlighted as being key to development effectiveness and cooperation.

1. Introduction

- **Angola and Switzerland work together to channel recovered assets worth $64 million to priority development needs.** In 2004 and 2012, Switzerland conducted separate criminal investigations into allegations of corruption and money laundering involving corrupt officials from Angola. In both, the proceeds were initially frozen ($21 million in 2004 and $43 million in 2012) as part of the criminal case. Although the criminal investigations were subsequently closed, the funds remained frozen, and it was not contested that the money belonged to the Angolan state. Switzerland and Angola explored options to return the funds and agreed to designate them for projects in key development areas. In 2004 the recovered assets financed projects that cleared land mines and supported agricultural development. In 2012 the funds were allocated for development needs that included establishment of a hospital infrastructure, water supply, and local capacity building for reintegration of displaced persons. Switzerland and Angola shared the planning and implementation responsibilities, and that helped Angola build capacity. The return has strengthened international cooperation and the capacity of law enforcement officials.

- **Following a settlement agreement, a £29.5 million ex-gratia payment is made for education needs in Tanzania. The U.K. Department for International Development plays a central role in project design.** In 2010 the company BAE Systems reached a settlement agreement with the U.K. Serious Fraud Office (SFO) regarding bribery allegations involving a $40 million contract to supply radar control systems to Tanzania. The company agreed to make voluntary reparations of £30 million (less fines imposed by the court) "for the benefit of the people of Tanzania."[1] Following advice and assistance from the U.K. Department for International Development (DFID), the government of Tanzania submitted a detailed proposal to dedicate the money to primary schools in the country, in particular for teaching materials and school desks, to rehabilitate classrooms, and to build teacher accommodations in rural, remote, and hard-to-reach areas. DFID facilitated exchanges between the government of Tanzania and the SFO and advised the government of Tanzania on the specifics of the proposal (e.g., advice on ring-fencing the payment for specific development objectives, setting up measurable development objectives, monitoring and evaluation, and drafting a good quality proposal). SFO and BAE accepted the proposal, and DFID continues to provide support to Tanzania in the expenditure of the funds.

---

1. Settlement Agreement between the Serious Fraud Office and BAE Systems PLC, dated February 2010 (accessed May 9, 2014), http://www.caat.org.uk/resources/companies/bae-systems/bae-settlement-basis-of -plea.pdf. See also *R v. BAE Systems PLC*, Case No.: S2010565, Crown Court at Southwark, December 21, 2010, http://www.judiciary.gov.uk/Resources/JCO/Documents/Judgments/r-v-bae-sentencing-remarks.pdf.

Corruption has a devastating impact on developing and transition countries. The cases described above demonstrate the impact that may come from a single corruption or bribery case. These are considerable amounts of money by any standard, but they are particularly devastating for poor countries.

Although estimates and methodologies for reaching them vary significantly, and have been criticized for flaws in technique, they provide an idea of the size of the problem. Even the more conservative of the approximations gathered by the Stolen Asset Recovery Initiative (StAR) in 2007 were staggering: $20 billion to $40 billion per year stolen by public officials from developing and transition jurisdictions. That is equivalent to 20 percent to 40 percent of flows of official development assistance (UN Office on Drugs and Crime and World Bank 2007, 9).

The return of the proceeds of corruption—asset recovery—can have a significant development impact. In the cases described at the beginning of the chapter, the proceeds recovered were used directly for development purposes—improvements in the health and education sectors and reintegration of displaced persons. In these and other cases, the benefits exceed the amounts returned, with additional benefits accruing in improved international cooperation and enhanced capacity of law enforcement and financial management officials.

Development agencies have a role in the asset recovery process. The BAE case provides an example of how development agencies can facilitate the return of stolen assets through compensation to victims. This report finds a number of other areas in which development agencies have played (or can play) a role, through policy influence, preventive measures, support of domestic law enforcement, or capacity building of foreign practitioners.

Development agencies and other bodies committed to improving development effectiveness should be interested in the asset recovery agenda, in view of their recognition that corruption undermines development efforts and international commitments to fight it and recover the proceeds. At the Fourth High Level Forum on Aid Effectiveness, held in Busan, Republic of Korea, in November 2011, more than 3,000 delegates met to review progress on implementing the principles of the Paris Declaration on Aid Effectiveness. The forum culminated in the signing of the Busan Partnership for Effective Development Co-operation ("Busan partnership") by ministers of developed and developing nations, emerging economies, providers of South-South and triangular cooperation, and civil society representatives. It was the first agreed framework for development cooperation involving such a variety of stakeholders.

Within this new framework, delegates committed themselves to fight corruption and to undertake efforts to identify, trace, freeze, and return the proceeds of corruption. Those commitments were not new to the development effectiveness agenda: the Third High Level Forum on Aid Effectiveness, held in Accra, Ghana, included similar commitments in the Accra Agenda for Action. Box 1.1 outlines those commitments. Although they are not new, the inclusion of these commitments in the Busan

The Busan Partnership for Effective Development Co-operation—Combating Corruption and Illicit Flows

33. Corruption is a plague that seriously undermines development globally, diverting resources that could be harnessed to finance development, damaging the quality of governance institutions, and threatening human security. It often fuels crime and contributes to conflict and fragility. We will intensify our joint efforts to fight corruption and illicit flows, consistent with the UN Convention against Corruption and other agreements to which we are party, such as the OECD Anti-Bribery Convention. To this end, we will:

a) Implement fully our respective commitments to eradicate corruption, enforcing our law and promoting a culture of zero tolerance for all corrupt practices. This includes efforts to improve fiscal transparency, strengthen independent enforcement mechanisms, and extend protection for whistle-blowers.

b) Accelerate our individual efforts to combat illicit financial flows by strengthening anti-money laundering measures, addressing tax evasion, and strengthening national and international policies, legal frameworks and institutional arrangements for the tracing, freezing, and recovery of illegal assets. This includes ensuring enactment and implementation of laws and practices that facilitate effective international co-operation.

The Accra Agenda for Action: Commitments to Fight Corruption

24. Transparency and accountability are essential elements for development results. They lie at the heart of the Paris Declaration, in which we agreed that countries and donors would become more accountable to each other and to their citizens. We will pursue these efforts by taking the following actions: [...]

d) Effective and efficient use of development financing requires both donors and partner countries to do their utmost to fight corruption. Donors and developing countries will respect the principles to which they have agreed, including those under the UN Convention against Corruption. Developing countries will address corruption by improving systems of investigation, legal redress, accountability and transparency in the use of public funds. *Donors will take steps in their own countries to combat corruption by individuals or corporations and to track, freeze, and recover illegally acquired assets.*

partnership is an important signal. Corruption is one of the few substantive issues addressed in the partnership agreement, which otherwise focuses almost exclusively on improving cooperation on international development. Their inclusion underlines the critical importance of combating corruption and recovering the proceeds for effective development.

Scope of the Report

This report measures the progress of Organisation for Economic Co-operation and Development (OECD) member countries in meeting their commitments to trace, freeze, seize, and recover the proceeds of corruption. It covers the period from January 2010 to June 2012 and follows an initial report measuring progress between 2006 and 2009, *Tracking Anti-Corruption and Asset Recovery Commitments: A Progress Report and Recommendations for Action* ("first StAR/OECD report"; StAR and OECD 2011). Progress was determined based on the level of law enforcement activity and reports of policy, institutional, and legislative measures taken by OECD members. Some of their challenges in meeting these commitments are described, along with good practices and recommendations to guide future efforts.

The report is primarily intended to support the anticorruption and asset recovery efforts of developed and developing jurisdictions, with a particular focus on actions for development agencies. Civil society organizations engaged in governance and development issues may wish to use the findings and recommendations in their reports and advocacy efforts as well.

Methodology

In reviewing OECD member progress on asset recovery between January 2010 and June 2012, the StAR/OECD team looked at data on corruption cases involving the tracing, freezing, or return of assets to a foreign jurisdiction (e.g., number of cases, value of assets frozen or returned, jurisdictions involved, etc.), as well as data on the policies, legal frameworks, and institutional arrangements that OECD countries have adopted to strengthen their asset recovery efforts.

The data were drawn primarily from a StAR/OECD Asset Recovery Questionnaire distributed to the 34 OECD members (see appendix C for the questionnaire). The team complemented those data with information from the StAR Asset Recovery Watch Database, the StAR settlement database, the first StAR/OECD report covering 2006–09, and independent research. A summary of this survey's results appeared in the OECD report "Illicit Financial Flows from Developing Countries: Measuring OECD Responses (2014)."

The questionnaires requested data on law enforcement efforts in freezing and returning assets, the sources of the cases, and the foreign jurisdictions where the assets originated. Given the scope of the report and previous difficulties collecting data on asset recovery, the questionnaires focused on high-level data and did not request specific information on the names of cases or progress in individual cases. A future survey may explore progress in that area. Information on policies, legal frameworks, and institutional arrangements adopted to strengthen asset recovery efforts was also requested. Responsibility for the accuracy of the information provided rests solely with the individual countries.

The StAR/OECD questionnaire was prepared in consultation with asset recovery practitioners from three OECD member countries. To facilitate the reporting effort, the questionnaires were pre-populated with data from the StAR Asset Recovery Database, and the countries were asked to review the pre-populated data and include any missing information.

Only 20 of the 34 countries responded. Responses were not received from Austria, Chile, Czech Republic, Estonia, Finland, Greece, Hungary, Iceland, Ireland, Korea, Mexico, Poland, Slovenia, and Turkey. Although previous responses from these countries and independent research suggest that it is unlikely that the overall picture of asset recovery cases would be much different than the one presented in this report had they responded, some data on policy, legislative, or institutional developments might have been missed. The low level of response may also be indicative of the priority given to the issue.

Terminology

In the questionnaire and in this report, "corruption offenses" are those outlined in articles 15–23 of the United Nations Convention against Corruption, or UNCAC, specifically, bribery of national public officials (art. 15); bribery of foreign public officials and officials of public international organizations (art. 16); embezzlement, misappropriation or other diversion of property by a public official (art. 17); trading in influence (art. 18); abuse of functions (art. 19); illicit enrichment (art. 20); bribery in the private sector (art. 21); embezzlement of property in the private sector (art. 22); and laundering proceeds of crime (art. 23).

"Asset recovery" is defined to include the powers envisaged in article 53–55 of UNCAC and is effectively the process by which proceeds of corruption are recovered and returned to a foreign jurisdiction. "Cases" are investigations, sanctions, acquittals, and settlement agreements.

Asset recovery is conducted through a variety of legal avenues, including criminal confiscation, non-conviction based confiscation, civil actions, and actions involving the use of mutual legal assistance. Regardless of the avenue selected, the objectives and fundamental process for asset recovery are generally as illustrated in figure 1.1.

Organization of the Report

This report is organized as follows: Chapter 2 provides some general observations on the data available; chapter 3 summarizes the main findings on asset recovery cases; chapters 4, 5, and 6 discuss the progress that countries have made in developing the necessary policy, legal, and institutional frameworks. Chapter 7 summarizes the role of developing countries in recovering the proceeds of corruption; chapter 8 reports on possible areas for the involvement of development agencies; and chapter 9 sets out the main

FIGURE 1.1 Process for Recovery of Stolen Assets

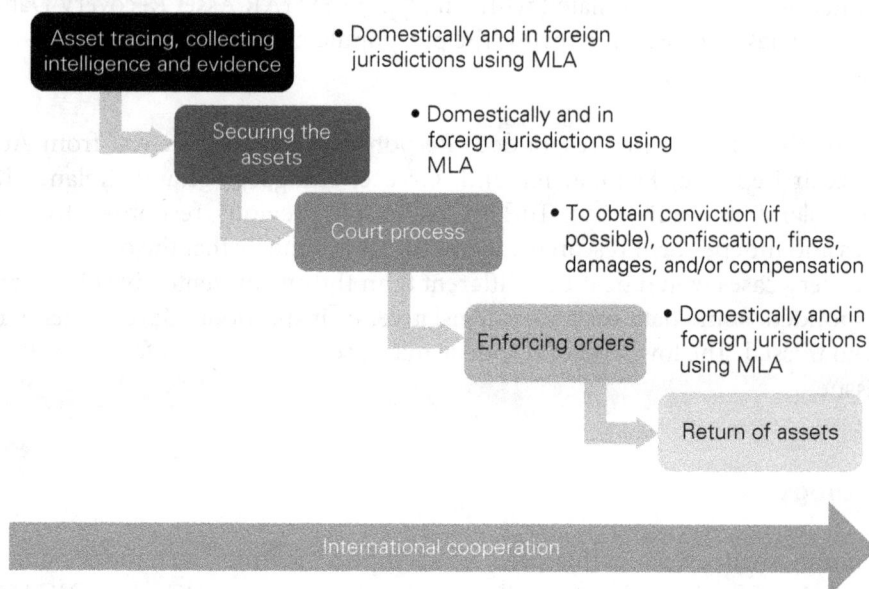

Asset tracing, collecting intelligence and evidence
- Domestically and in foreign jurisdictions using MLA

Securing the assets
- Domestically and in foreign jurisdictions using MLA

Court process
- To obtain conviction (if possible), confiscation, fines, damages, and/or compensation

Enforcing orders
- Domestically and in foreign jurisdictions using MLA

Return of assets

International cooperation

Source: Authors' illustration based on Brun et al. 2011, 6.
Note: MLA = Mutual legal assistance.

conclusions of the report. Three appendixes summarize report recommendations, show the G20 principles on asset recovery, and reproduce the StAR/OECD questionnaire.

References

Brun, J. P., L. Gray, C. Scott, and K. M. Stephenson. 2011. *Asset Recovery Handbook: A Guide for Practitioners.* Washington, DC: World Bank.

StAR and OECD (Stolen Asset Recovery Initiative and Organisation for Economic Co-operation and Development). 2011. *Tracking Anti-Corruption and Asset Recovery Commitments: A Progress Report and Recommendations for Action.* Paris: OECD. http://www.oecd.org.dac/governance-development/49263968.pdf or www.worldbank.org/star.

UN Office on Drugs and Crime and World Bank Group. 2007. *Stolen Asset Recovery Initiative: Challenges, Opportunities, and Action Plan,* 9. Washington, DC: World Bank.

OECD (2014). *Illicit Financial Flows from Developing Countries: Measuring OECD Responses.* Paris. available at http://dx.doi.org/10.1787/9789264203501-en.

Paris Declaration on Aid Effectiveness available at http://dx.doi.org/10.1787/9789264098084-en.

The Busan Partnership for Effective Development Cooperation. http://dx.doi.org/10.1787/9789264203501-en.

The Accra Agenda for Action. http://www.oecd.org/dac/effectiveness/34428351.pdf.

2. General Observations on the Data

Transparency and accountability are essential elements for developmental results.
—Accra Agenda for Action

StAR/OECD used two main sources of data in examining OECD member progress on tracing, freezing, and recovering assets. The first source was data on the policies, legal frameworks, and institutional arrangements that countries have adopted to strengthen their asset recovery efforts. The second was data from law enforcement on the number of cases conducted; the value of assets traced, frozen, confiscated, and recovered; the jurisdictions involved; mechanisms used (e.g., criminal confiscation, non-conviction based confiscation); and what prompted the action. For example, was a freeze initiated pursuant to a mutual legal assistance (MLA) request, a domestic investigation, or an administrative order?

Overall, little information was available on law enforcement cases. Most responding countries indicated that they were unable to provide a complete set of such data. They cited a number of reasons, which can be categorized into two main challenges.

In the first category, a broader data set was being collected within which it was not possible to differentiate corruption and asset recovery cases. The broader data set may be collected for domestic or international evaluations (such as domestic asset recovery offices, the OECD Working Group on Bribery, the Financial Action Task Force, or the UNCAC Conference of States Parties) but may lack the specifics to identify asset recovery cases. In some cases, data may be collected on all assets frozen and confiscated but without identification of the underlying offense or wrongdoing, for example, whether the funds were the proceeds of corruption, drug-related offenses, tax crimes, or other crime. Or the data may not show whether the freeze or confiscation was due to a domestic or a foreign case. Data may be collected on money-laundering cases and related confiscations but without specifics on the predicate crime. In other words, the data collected do not distinguish recovery of the proceeds of corruption from the proceeds of other types of offenses.

The second category includes cases in which law enforcement data are not collected in the first place. This happens in countries where cases are conducted at cantonal, state, or provincial level; in private civil actions in which the government is not a party; or when a number of different agencies have the authority to investigate and prosecute such cases. Cases may be conducted and private civil actions may be pursued, but the data are not being collected at a central level. In these situations, the only cases that might be reported are those that come to the attention of national-level authorities, whether through federal prosecutions or mutual legal assistance (MLA) requests. That leaves out asset freezes that may take place at an administrative or informal cooperation level, as well as direct recoveries ordered by courts. Other reasons cited for not collecting the data were their sensitive nature, a lack of enabling legislation, and a lack of resources.

A major challenge in data collection was the low level of response on the part of many OECD members. Of the 34 OECD members, the aforementioned 14 did not respond to the survey at all (see chapter 1). Many of the countries that responded provided incomplete information and did not respond to follow-up questions, even where the additional information would increase their results (for example, the seizure of Equatorial Guinea assets by France could not be confirmed and so could not be included).[1]

These issues are not new. The first StAR/OECD report noted similar problems with data collection (StAR and OECD, 2011, 19–21). Nor are the problems of data collection confined to asset recovery cases. Similar issues have been reported by countries gathering enforcement data for the OECD Working Group on Bribery, countries reporting on money laundering cases, and so on.

Gathering data is important. Statistics play a major function in domestic decision making and in how resources are used in all areas of government, including taxation, health care, education, fighting crime, or development assistance. Data and statistics are also important measuring the effectiveness of strategies, laws, and institutional frameworks. Does the system work? Are there results in terms of assets frozen or returned? Evidence that the system is working (or not working) is essential information that can guide decision makers in thinking strategically on priorities, closing gaps, and efficient resource allocation.

In addition, experience has demonstrated that where asset recovery is given a low priority and ineffective laws or institutions result, criminals will exploit those vulnerabilities to launder their corruption proceeds.

At the international level, standard setting-bodies focused on results and effectiveness are increasingly emphasizing gathering statistics. The Financial Action Task Force (FATF), for example, has adopted an assessment methodology that looks equally at the effectiveness of AML/CFT systems (anti-money laundering and combating the financing of terrorism) and technical compliance (whether laws and institutions are in place) (FATF 2013). As countries are assessed against this standard, assembling comprehensive statistics will become more and more important for countries to demonstrate their effectiveness. Similarly, the OECD Working Group on Bribery collects law enforcement

---

1. See StAR Asset Recovery Watch, "Teodoro Nguema Obiang Mbasogo/Teodoro Nguema Obiang Mangue (France)," available at http://star.worldbank.org/corruption-cases/node/18584. See also Des, Car News, "11 Supercars of Teodoro Obiang Nguema Mbasogo Seized by French Police," September 29, 2011, available at http://www.gtspirit.com/2011/09/29/11-supercars-of-teodoro-obiang-nguema-mbasogo-seized-by-french-police/.

data on bribery cases, and the UNCAC (United Nations Convention against Corruption) review mechanism collects data on UNCAC implementation.

International organizations and other entities requesting data can do their part to make the number of data requests less burdensome by collaborating on requests for data, as StAR and OECD have done in producing this report, or by producing indicators that countries can use in measuring results. For example, the European Commission indicated in an internal strategy document that it will develop common indicators against which member states can evaluate the performance of asset recovery offices (European Commission 2010, 6). Where countries have made international commitments on fighting corruption and recovering its proceeds, there should be a corresponding interest in determining whether they are effective in fulfilling them.

Several ideas for improving data collection emerged from the information provided by OECD members for this report:

- *Start with some data gathering, then expand.* All countries experience difficulties with gathering data. Some of the 20 countries that responded to the StAR questionnaire were able to produce a selection of data, even though it was incomplete. The others did not provide any law enforcement data at all, citing various data collection problems, despite indications from public sources that cases occurred. Even incomplete data can be helpful in showing some level of progress, indicating good practices, and so forth. Therefore all countries should aim to gather the "low-hanging fruit"—data that are easy to obtain or from agencies where results might be expected. Once the process is initiated and under way, countries can proceed to other data sets and identify and fill gaps.
- *Develop a system to flag asset recovery cases among broader sets of data already being collected.* For example, previously in the United Kingdom, cases involving the recovery of proceeds of corruption could not be extracted as a separate class. A new system introduced in 2011 now allows for the tagging of cases involving foreign assets, so that corruption cases involving foreign assets can be counted separately.
- *Incorporate a data collection objective into asset recovery policies, and ensure that adequate resources are made available.* A number of countries indicated that they lacked resources and enabling legislation. But if countries are serious about ensuring the policies they set are effective, they should include data gathering to reveal those policies' impact. For example, the Netherlands Criminal Asset Deprivation Bureau (BOOM) has set data collection as an objective of the bureau, committing itself to collecting data on all asset recovery cases.
- *Critically evaluate generalizations that data are "too sensitive" to collect. If a sensitive case is identified, consider releasing "sanitized" data.* Although the content of ongoing investigations and prosecutions is sensitive in nature, countries can provide general statistical data without compromising a case, such as the number of cases and the value of assets that have been frozen, confiscated, or returned. All countries that responded were able to provide those general statistics. They also provided the names of the foreign jurisdictions involved in all but four cases. In those four, Belgium, the Netherlands, and the United Kingdom identified progress in

terms of the value of assets being frozen, but because of concerns that releasing the data could compromise a case, they deleted the name of the jurisdiction involved. Thus they could report progress, yet also protect sensitive case information. The data on the specific jurisdiction can be entered once the case is finalized.

- *Make laws, policies, institutional changes, and data on case achievements publicly available and accessible through a central source.* Publishing information on domestic asset recovery efforts in one location or publication will help to highlight a country's commitments to asset recovery and can be a good resource for requesting countries. For example, Switzerland has published its laws, case examples, and policies on a website (see figure 2.1). Such efforts will also contribute to the transparency and accountability commitments of countries in the Paris Declaration, Accra Agenda for Action and the Busan Partnership.

Recommendation:

Developed and developing countries should maintain comprehensive statistics on asset recovery cases, including assets frozen or confiscated, reparations or restitution ordered, and assets returned. Gaps in the data should be identified and their collection addressed. Where possible, countries should gather data on the various means to return assets, including criminal and non-conviction based confiscation, administrative confiscation, private civil actions, or other forms of direct recovery. Statistics on cases and information on laws and results should be publicly available and accessible at a central location such as a website.

FIGURE 2.1 Laws, Policies, and Data on Cases Available on the Swiss Government Website

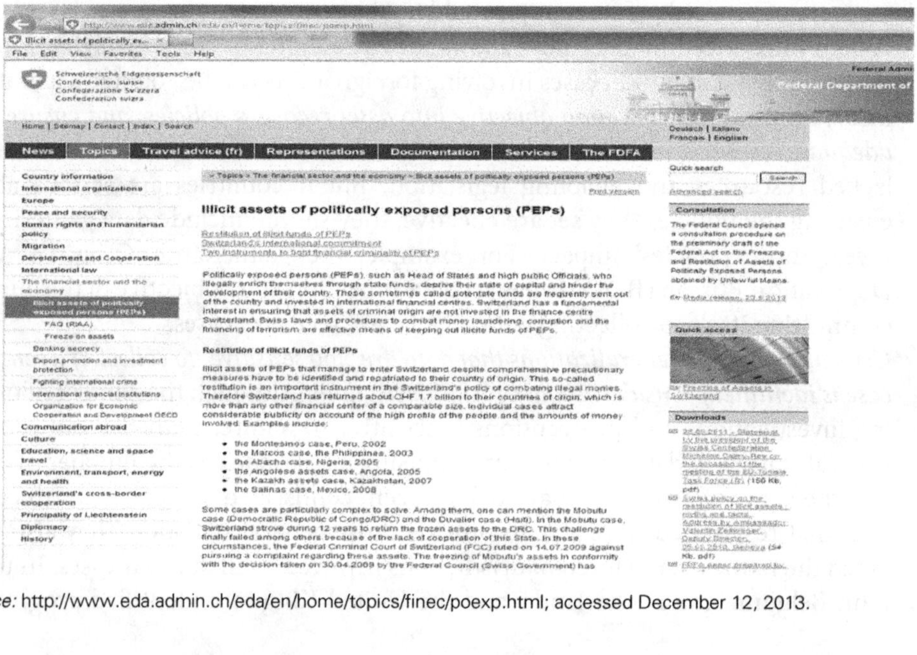

Source: http://www.eda.admin.ch/eda/en/home/topics/finec/poexp.html; accessed December 12, 2013.

References

European Commission. 2010. "Communication from the Commission to the European Parliament and the Council: The EU Internal Strategy in Action: Five Steps towards a More Secure Europe." COM (2010) 673 of 22.11.2010, Brussels.

FATF (Financial Action Task Force). 2013. *Methodology for Assessing Technical Compliance with the FATF Recommendations and Effectiveness of AML/CFT Systems.* Paris: FATF.

StAR/OECD. 2011. *Tracking Anti-Corruption and Asset Recovery Commitments: A Progress Report and Recommendations for Action.* Paris: OECD. http://www.oecd .org.dac/governance-development/49263968.pdf and www.worldbank.org/star.

3. Progress on Cases: Tracing, Freezing, and Recovering Proceeds of Corruption

The StAR/OECD questionnaire requested data in the following areas:

- The number of cases of assets traced, frozen, or returned and value of assets;
- The foreign jurisdiction (or country harmed by corruption);
- The source of the case, such as mutual legal assistance (MLA), domestic investigation, or governmental order, decree, or law; and
- The method used to freeze or return the assets, such as criminal or non-conviction based (NCB) confiscation, private civil action, domestic investigation, or reparations following a settlement.

A total of 41 cases were reported by eight countries—Belgium, Canada, Luxembourg, the Netherlands, Portugal, Switzerland, United Kingdom, and the United States. Of these, 29 cases involved the freezing or seizing of assets and 12 were returns.

Similar to experience with the first StAR/OECD report, the data on asset tracing investigations remain extremely limited. Only Luxemburg, the Netherlands, Portugal, and the United States provided information on tracing efforts, with a value of $166 million. The remaining countries cited problems with data collection or sensitive information. In addition, the values reported were equivalent to the assets frozen by those countries. Inasmuch as the value of assets traced should, at least in theory, be equal to or greater than the value of assets frozen or seized (a country has to trace the assets it freezes or seizes and may pursue some tracing investigations that do not result in an asset freeze or seizure), these numbers offer little in terms of value added and risk double-counting of data.

Overall the data provided were sufficient to support a number of findings or trends, in particular compared to the first StAR/OECD report. This chapter describes those findings. Chapters 4, 5 and 6 discuss the findings related to the policy, legislative, and institutional changes.

OECD Members Pursuing Cases

More countries are pursuing asset recovery cases involving assets in foreign jurisdictions, but the overall number of OECD members doing so remains small. Since the first StAR/OECD report, four new countries—Belgium, Canada, the Netherlands, and Portugal—have joined the list of OECD members that have frozen corruption proceeds,

TABLE 3.1	OECD Members Pursuing Stolen Asset Recovery Cases Involving Foreign Proceeds, 2010–June 2012		
Countries pursuing cases	No reported cases	Did not respond to the survey	
Belgium	Australia[a]	Austria	
Canada	Denmark	Chile	
Luxembourg	France[a]	Czech Republic	
Netherlands	Germany	Estonia	
Portugal	Israel	Finland	
Switzerland	Italy	Greece	
United Kingdom	Japan	Hungary	
United States	New Zealand	Iceland	
	Norway	Ireland	
	Slovak Republic	Korea, Rep.	
	Spain	Mexico	
	Sweden	Poland	
		Slovenia	
		Turkey	

Source: Authors' compilation based on responses to StAR/OECD survey.
a. Australia and France reported cases in the first StAR/OECD report.

bringing the number up to 10. The remaining countries did not report cases that met the criteria for this report (table 3.1; see table 3A.1, at the end of this chapter, for additional details).

Value of Assets Frozen and Returned by OECD Members

Although there has been an increase in the value of assets frozen, the value of assets returned remains at a level similar to that found by the first StAR/OECD report. Belgium, Canada, Luxembourg, the Netherlands, Portugal, Switzerland, the United Kingdom, and the United States reported 29 freezing cases, totaling $1.398 billion, between 2010 and 2012. This activity over a 2.5-year period is already slightly greater than over the 4-year period covered by the first StAR/OECD report (20 cases of $1.225 billion), demonstrating increased activity in the freezing of assets.

Only Switzerland, the United Kingdom, and the United States reported returns in the same period, a total of 12 cases valued at $147.2 million (see figure 3.3). The value of assets returned over the 2.5-year period is a little over half of the value of assets returned over the four years from 2006 to 2009 ($276.3 million), showing a rate of asset returns slightly lower than that found by the first StAR/OECD report.

Figure 3.1 shows OECD country reports of total assets frozen and returned to foreign jurisdictions during the period 2010 to June 2012 and the comparable reports from the first StAR/OECD report, covering 2006–09; and figures 3.2 and 3.3 shows reports for the entire period of 2006 to June 2012.

FIGURE 3.1

OECD Country Reports of Assets Frozen and Assets Returned to Foreign Jurisdictions, Seperated by Reporting Periods
Millions of dollars

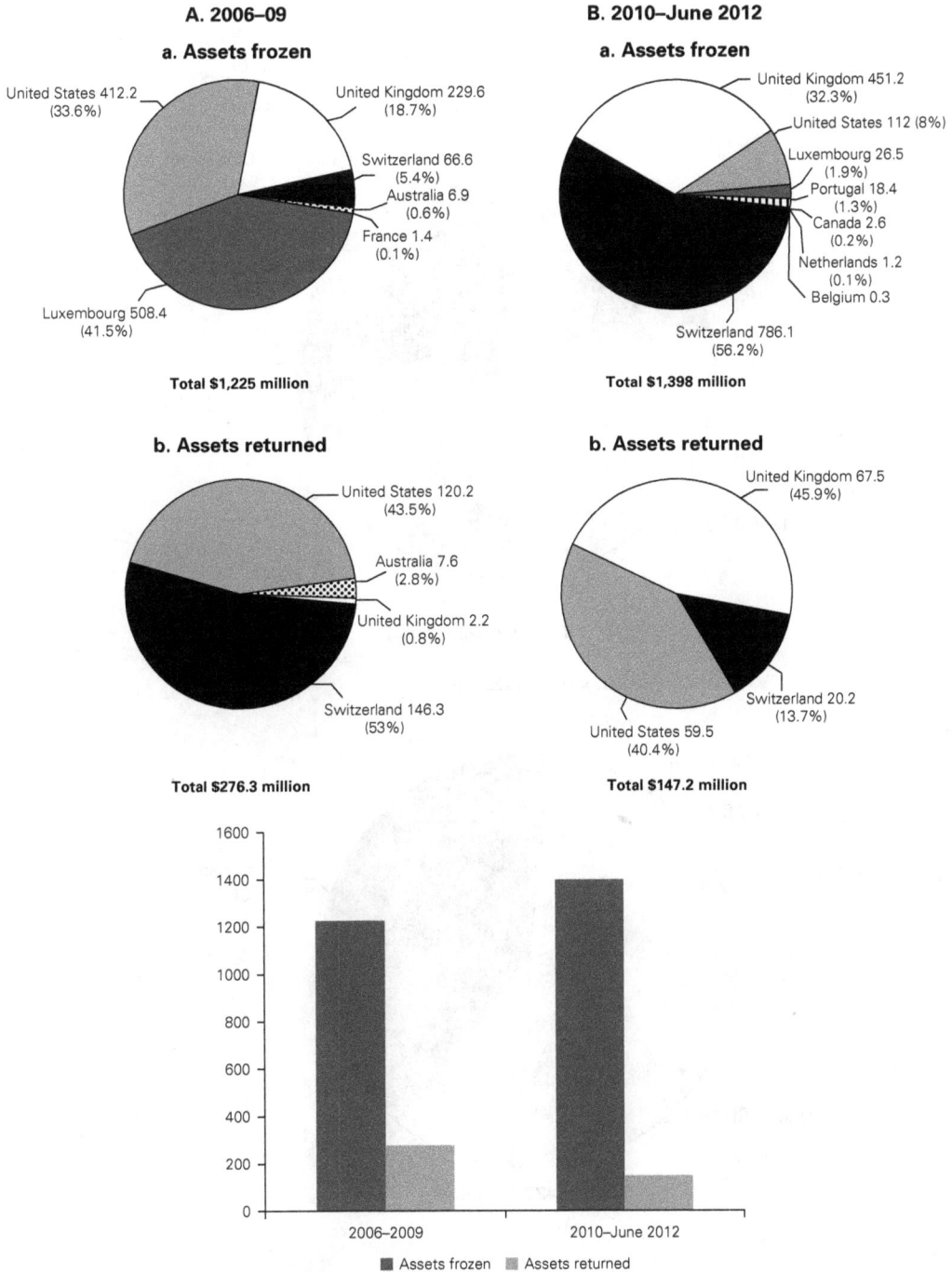

A. 2006–09

a. Assets frozen

United States 412.2
(33.6%)

United Kingdom 229.6
(18.7%)

Switzerland 66.6
(5.4%)

Australia 6.9
(0.6%)

France 1.4
(0.1%)

Luxembourg 508.4
(41.5%)

Total $1,225 million

B. 2010–June 2012

a. Assets frozen

United Kingdom 451.2
(32.3%)

United States 112 (8%)

Luxembourg 26.5
(1.9%)

Portugal 18.4
(1.3%)

Canada 2.6
(0.2%)

Netherlands 1.2
(0.1%)

Belgium 0.3

Switzerland 786.1
(56.2%)

Total $1,398 million

b. Assets returned

United States 120.2
(43.5%)

Australia 7.6
(2.8%)

United Kingdom 2.2
(0.8%)

Switzerland 146.3
(53%)

Total $276.3 million

b. Assets returned

United Kingdom 67.5
(45.9%)

Switzerland 20.2
(13.7%)

United States 59.5
(40.4%)

Total $147.2 million

	2006–2009	2010–June 2012
■ Assets frozen		
■ Assets returned		

Sources: (A) StAR and OECD 2011; and (B) Authors' compilation based on responses to StAR/OECD survey.

FIGURE 3.2

OECD Country Reports of Assets Frozen and Assets Returned to Foreign Jurisdictions, Combined Totals 2006–June 2012 Summary
Millions of dollars

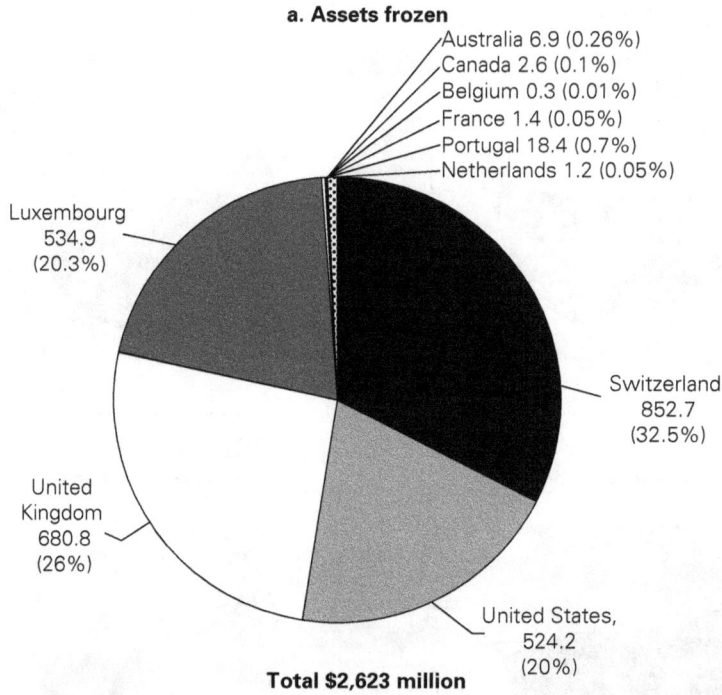

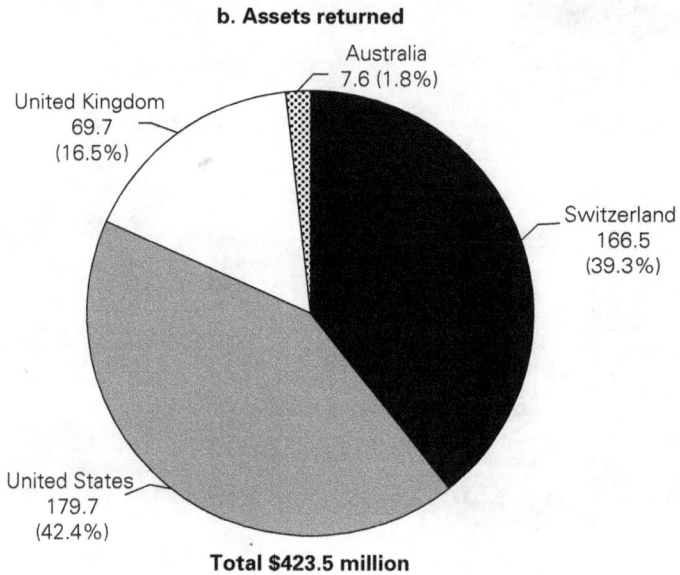

a. Assets frozen

Australia 6.9 (0.26%)
Canada 2.6 (0.1%)
Belgium 0.3 (0.01%)
France 1.4 (0.05%)
Portugal 18.4 (0.7%)
Netherlands 1.2 (0.05%)

Luxembourg
534.9
(20.3%)

Switzerland
852.7
(32.5%)

United
Kingdom
680.8
(26%)

United States,
524.2
(20%)

Total $2,623 million

b. Assets returned

Australia
7.6 (1.8%)

United Kingdom
69.7
(16.5%)

Switzerland
166.5
(39.3%)

United States
179.7
(42.4%)

Total $423.5 million

FIGURE 3.3 Total Value of Assets Frozen and Returned 2006–June 2012
Millions of dollars

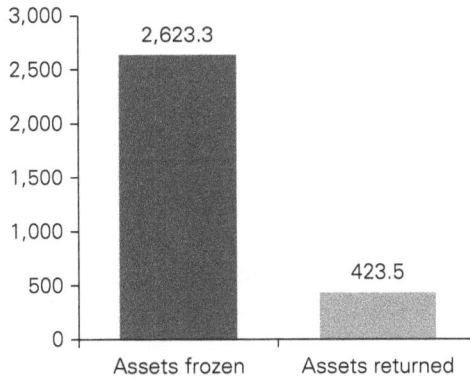

Source: Authors' compilation based on responses to StAR/OECD survey and StAR and OECD 2011.

Figure 3.3 shows that assets returned were significantly less than assets frozen. The total value of assets returned between 2006 and June 2012 was $423.5 million, which is significantly less than the $2.623 billion in assets frozen. These totals are a fraction of the estimated $20 billion to $40 billion stolen each year from developing and transition jurisdictions.

Since the StAR/OECD survey collected general data on assets frozen or returned, it is not possible to follow the activity in specific cases. However, the general data gathered mirrors the experiences that jurisdictions have reported anecdotally on individual cases. News media reports of assets stolen and hidden in particular jurisdictions have cited much higher values than the values traced. In turn, those values are much greater than the amounts that can eventually be frozen, confiscated (or ordered to be paid as damages or a fine by a court), and returned. Figure 3.4 illustrates this trajectory.

FIGURE 3.4   Illustration of Trends in Asset Recovery Cases (Anecdotal)

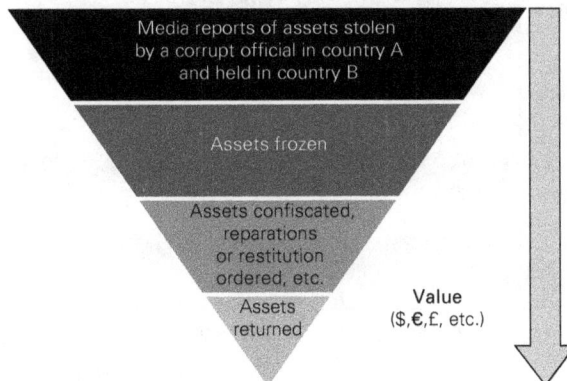

Source: Authors' compilation.

Drilling down further to the country level, some countries have reported activity in terms of assets frozen, yet no assets have been returned. The lengthy time it takes to recover assets may explain the lack of returns following the more recent freezes, such as those by Belgium, Canada, the Netherlands, and Portugal. For asset freezes reported prior to 2010, the results are more mixed. Australia, Switzerland, the United Kingdom, and the United States reported returns, but France and Luxembourg reported none. This difference is most striking in the case of Luxembourg, where $535.4 million has been reported frozen—the third-highest value reported—but no assets have been returned. Although it is possible that these cases have not been resolved to the extent that a return is possible, other countries with similar activity levels have had at least some progress to report in assets returned (see figure 3.5).

The value of assets frozen does not include Libyan assets frozen pursuant to United Nations Security Council Resolutions (UNSCR) 1970 (2011) and 1973 (2011). Those resolutions

| FIGURE 3.5 | Assets Frozen and Returned, by OECD Country, 2006–June 2012 |
| | *Millions of dollars* |

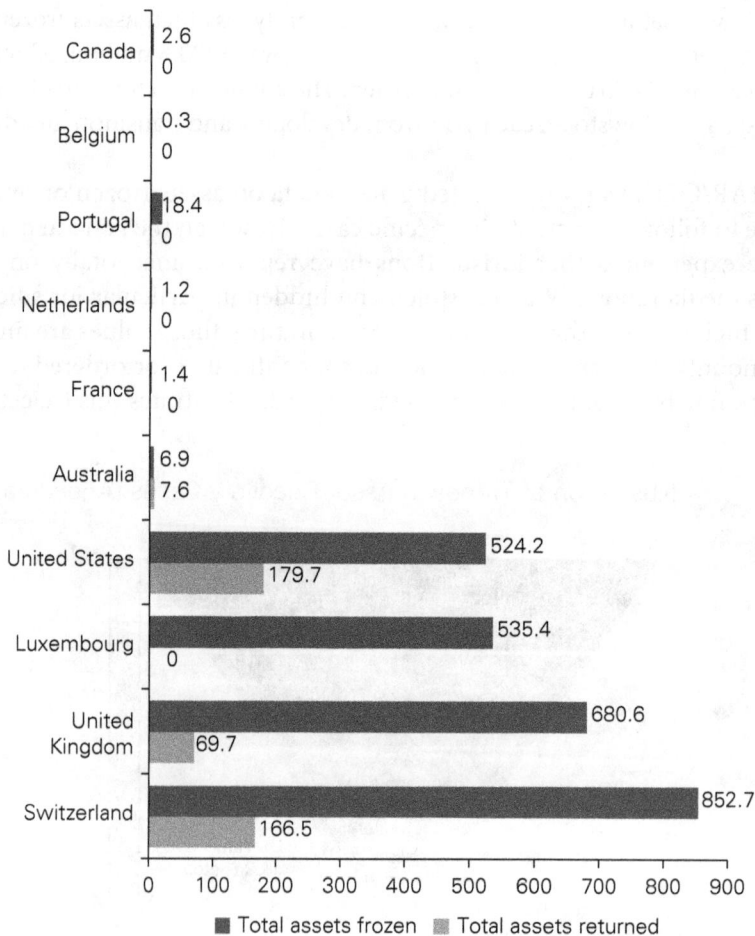

Source: Authors' compilation based on responses to StAR/OECD survey.
Note: The remaining OECD members did not report cases of assets frozen or returned.

FIGURE 3.6 Libyan Asset Freezes Reported by Four OECD Members, 2010–June 2012

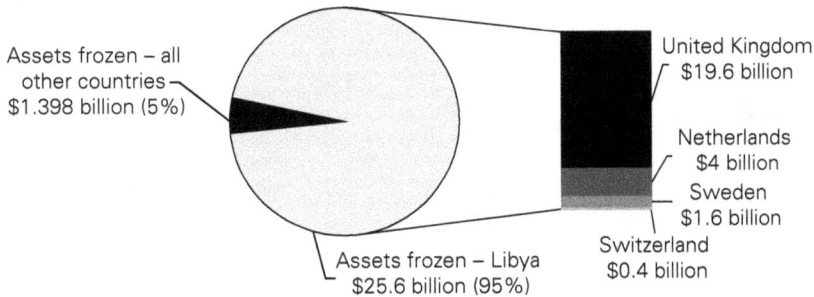

Assets frozen – all other countries $1.398 billion (5%)

United Kingdom $19.6 billion

Netherlands $4 billion

Sweden $1.6 billion

Switzerland $0.4 billion

Assets frozen – Libya $25.6 billion (95%)

Source: Authors' compilation based on responses to StAR/OECD survey.

imposed a freeze on a broad range of assets belonging to the Libyan government (such as the Central Bank, Libyan Investment Authority, and Libyan National Oil Corporation), not exclusively on the proceeds of corruption. Assets were frozen worldwide, including $25.6 billion reported to StAR/OECD by the Netherlands, Sweden, Switzerland, and the United Kingdom. The list is likely to grow, given that some countries did not consider Libyan asset freezes to be covered by this report or were not able to provide estimates.

Although some of those Libyan assets may have involved the proceeds of corruption, it is impossible to distinguish them, and therefore the data could not be included in the StAR/OECD data set. In addition, where the UN Security Council has lifted a freeze, the funds are released to the owner which may be a state-owned entity or an individual. If an individual, the funds were returned to the individual and not to Libya. As illustrated in figure 3.6, the expansive scope of the freezes would dwarf the value of all other asset freezes reported to StAR/OECD.

Jurisdictions Where the Proceeds Originated

In almost all of the 41 cases reported, OECD members named the jurisdiction where the proceeds originated. There were only three cases in which the name of the jurisdiction was redacted because of the sensitive nature of the case. Thus the data in the maps in figures 3.7 and 3.8 provide a good picture of the jurisdictions and proceeds involved.

OECD members have made significant progress in expanding the freezing and return of stolen assets beyond developed countries.

Between 2006 and 2009, the majority of asset freezing or recovery cases involved other developed countries. Only 11 developing countries fell outside this group, accounting for less than 40 percent of assets frozen and returned. Those countries were Belarus, Brazil, China, Indonesia, Kazakhstan, Mexico, Nigeria, Peru, South Africa, Uganda, and Ukraine (StAR and OECD 2011, 31–32).

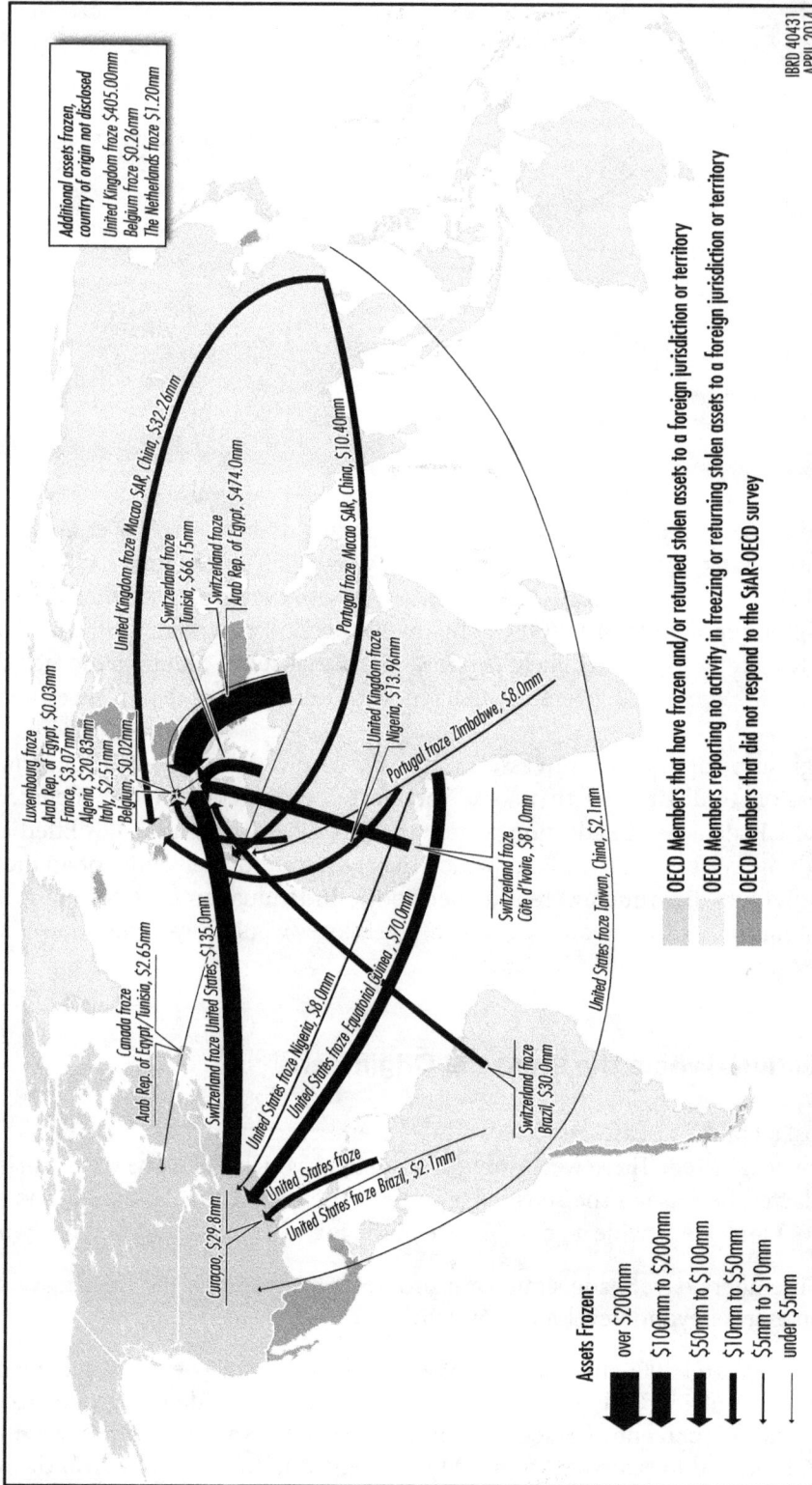

Additional assets frozen,
country of origin not disclosed
United Kingdom froze $405.00mm
Belgium froze $0.26mm
The Netherlands froze $1.20mm

United Kingdom froze Macao SAR, China, $32.26mm

Switzerland froze
Tunisia, $66.15mm

Switzerland froze
Arab Rep. of Egypt, $474.0mm

Portugal froze Macao SAR, China, $10.40mm

Luxembourg froze
Arab Rep. of Egypt, $0.03mm
France, $3.07mm
Algeria, $20.83mm
Italy, $2.51mm
Belgium, $0.02mm

United Kingdom froze
Nigeria, $13.96mm

Portugal froze Zimbabwe, $8.0mm

Switzerland froze
Côte d'Ivoire, $81.0mm

Canada froze
Arab Rep. of Egypt/Tunisia, $2.65mm

Switzerland froze United States, $135.0mm

United States froze Nigeria, $8.0mm

United States froze Equatorial Guinea, $70.0mm

United States froze Taiwan, China, $2.1mm

Switzerland froze
Brazil, $30.0mm

United States froze
Curaçao, $29.8mm

United States froze Brazil, $2.1mm

IBRD 40431
APRIL 2014

Assets Frozen:
over $200mm
$100mm to $200mm
$50mm to $100mm
$10mm to $50mm
$5mm to $10mm
under $5mm

OECD Members that have frozen and/or returned stolen assets to a foreign jurisdiction or territory

OECD Members reporting no activity in freezing or returning stolen assets to a foreign jurisdiction or territory

OECD Members that did not respond to the StAR-OECD survey

(continued next page)

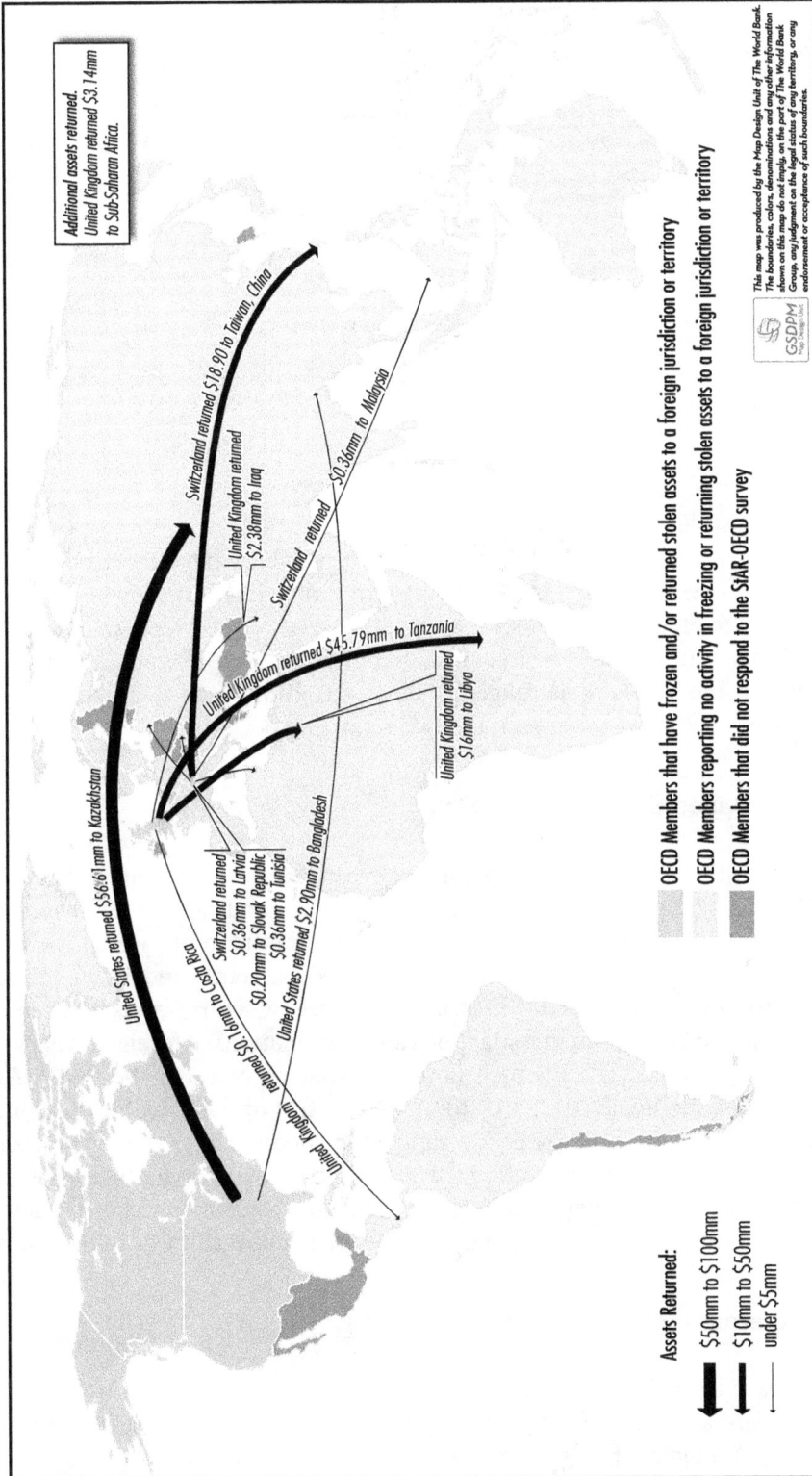

Additional assets returned.
United Kingdom returned $3.14mm to Sub-Saharan Africa.

Switzerland returned $18.90 to Taiwan, China

United Kingdom returned $2.38mm to Iraq

Switzerland returned $0.36mm to Malaysia

United Kingdom returned $45.79mm to Tanzania

United States returned $56.61mm to Kazakhstan

United Kingdom returned $0.16mm to Costa Rica

Switzerland returned $0.36mm to Latvia
$0.20mm to Slovak Republic
$0.36mm to Tunisia
United States returned $2.90mm to Bangladesh

United Kingdom returned $16mm to Libya

OECD Members that have frozen and/or returned stolen assets to a foreign jurisdiction or territory

OECD Members reporting no activity in freezing or returning stolen assets to a foreign jurisdiction or territory

OECD Members that did not respond to the StAR-OECD survey

This map was produced by the Map Design Unit of The World Bank.
The boundaries, colors, denominations and any other information
shown on this map do not imply, on the part of The World Bank
Group, any judgment on the legal status of any territory, or any
endorsement or acceptance of such boundaries.

GSDPM
Map Design Unit

Assets Returned:

$50mm to $100mm

$10mm to $50mm

under $5mm

Source: Authors' compilation based on responses to StAR/OECD survey.

FIGURE 3.9 Increases in Asset Freezing or Recovery Cases with Developing Countries between 2006 and June 2012
In millions of dollars

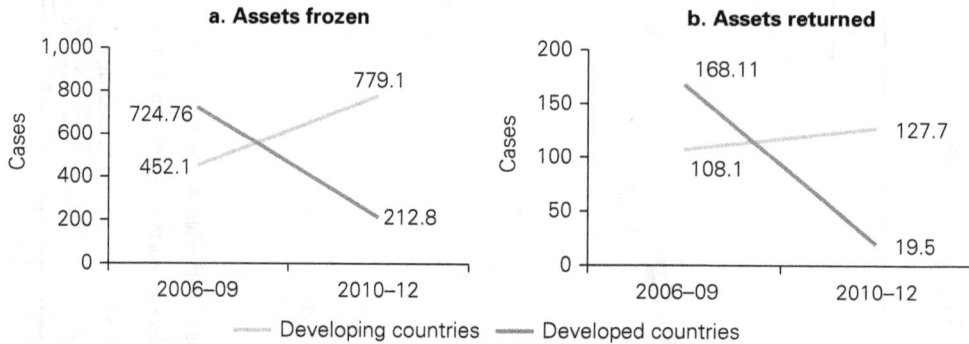

a. Assets frozen

724.76
452.1
779.1
212.8

Cases

2006–09   2010–12

b. Assets returned

168.11
108.1
127.7
19.5

Cases

2006–09   2010–12

- - - - Developing countries   ——— Developed countries

Source: Authors' compilation based on responses to StAR/OECD survey.

Between 2010 and June 2012, however, those numbers have increased significantly. Assets were frozen or returned to 15 developing countries and comprised 80 percent of the total value of assets frozen and returned. The countries were Algeria, Bangladesh, Brazil, Costa Rica, Côte d'Ivoire, Arab Republic of Egypt, Equatorial Guinea, Iraq, Kazakhstan, Libya, Malaysia, Nigeria, Tanzania, Tunisia, and Zimbabwe. Figure 3.9 shows the progress made between the two reporting periods.

How Are Cases Being Initiated?

Proactive initiatives by OECD member governments or law enforcement agencies remain important sources for successful asset freezes and returns. Only four countries provided data on the sources of freezes or returns, but the results were noteworthy. One country relied exclusively on formal mutual legal assistance requests to freeze assets, but the others applied proactive measures to freeze or return assets. Law enforcement agencies initiated their own investigations and prosecutions of foreign bribery or money laundering (or both) in a manner similar to that reported in the first StAR/OECD report (StAR and OECD 2011, 25–26). In the context of the Arab Spring, some OECD member governments also passed laws and issued decrees to proactively freeze assets of corrupt leaders rather than waiting for a formal request for mutual legal assistance. Chapter 5 provides further detail on the legal mechanisms used to proactively take action in conducting cases, initiating international cooperation, and freezing assets.

Legal Avenues for Asset Recovery

The results of the StAR/OECD survey show that OECD members are using multiple avenues to freeze and recover the proceeds of corruption. The methods go beyond what is commonly thought of as the traditional method for asset recovery, a criminal confiscation case.

Administrative asset freezes in connection with the Arab Spring brought impressive results. Of the total assets reported frozen by OECD members, 39 percent originated in either Tunisia or Arab Republic of Egypt ($542.8 million of the total $1.398 billion). The assets were frozen pursuant to decrees or laws passed by Canada, the European Union, and Switzerland and not based on MLA requests (see box 4.4, in the next chapter, for a description of these laws). Their value is likely to be higher, given that Libyan corruption proceeds could not be included because they could not be distinguished from the broader Libyan asset freezes described above.

For asset returns, countries used multiple legal avenues, including criminal and non-conviction based confiscation, criminal reparations and restitution, and private civil actions. Reports by OECD members show that criminal confiscation accounted for only 13 percent of the total assets returned (see figure 3.10). Other avenues were far more productive, in particular non-conviction based (NCB) confiscation (40 percent of returns) and criminal restitution and reparations (34 percent). Assets were also returned following private civil actions in the United Kingdom by Libya (11 percent of returns) and Ukraine (value unknown).

Of the 12 asset return cases, 8 were resolved by settlement agreements, accounting for 74 percent of the total value of assets returned (figure 3.11). Although that result demonstrates that the method is gaining traction as a means for resolving foreign bribery cases in civil and common law jurisdictions, the need exists to discuss further

FIGURE 3.10 Legal Avenues Used for Asset Recovery, 2010–June 2012
Millions of dollars

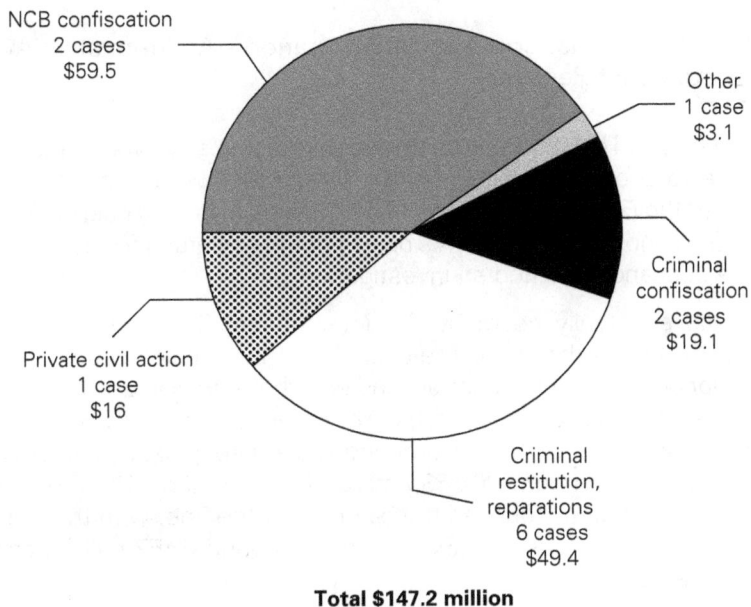

NCB confiscation
2 cases
$59.5

Other
1 case
$3.1

Criminal
confiscation
2 cases
$19.1

Criminal
restitution,
reparations
6 cases
$49.4

Private civil action
1 case
$16

Total $147.2 million

Source: Authors' compilation based on responses to StAR/OECD survey.
Note: NCB = non-conviction based.

expansion of asset recovery via settlement agreements, considering the huge size and types of monetary sanctions imposed in settlement cases (see also chapter 5).

Another innovative means for recovery of assets was an international arbitration case initiated by Taiwan, China, at the International Chamber of Commerce Court of Arbitration (see box 3.1).

| FIGURE 3.11 | Assets Returned Pursuant to a Settlement Agreement, 2010–June 2012 |

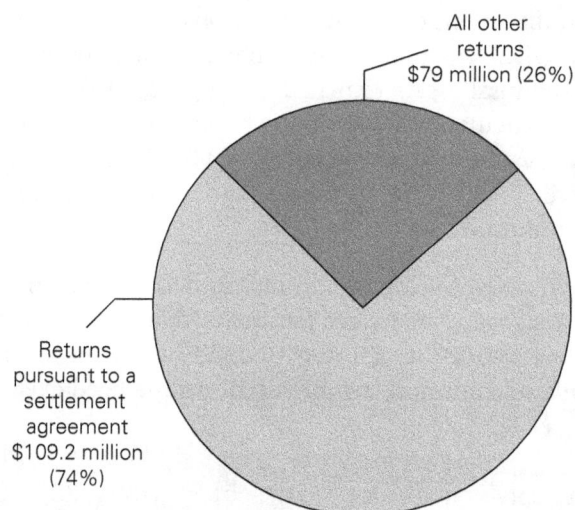

All other
returns
$79 million (26%)

Returns
pursuant to a
settlement
agreement
$109.2 million
(74%)

Source: Authors' compilation based on responses to StAR/OECD survey.

| BOX 3.1 | International Commercial Arbitration—An Innovative Avenue for Asset Recovery |

In 1991, France and Taiwan, China, signed a contract to supply six Lafayette Class frigates for a total of $2.5 billion. Shortly thereafter, the authorities in Taiwan, China accused the French state-owned Elf Aquitaine of having paid bribes through the French firm Thomson CSF (now Thales Group) to persuade the authorities to approve the deal and launched an investigation.

The case was eventually heard by the International Chamber of Commerce's International Court of Arbitration. The court found that Thales Group had violated the anticorruption terms of the contract and was therefore liable to repay all bribes, plus associated interest and legal fees. Thales appealed, and the decision was upheld by the Paris Court of Appeal, ordering Thales Group to pay compensation to Taiwan, China, in the amount of €630 million ($913 million). The French government and Thales Group announced the payment of the fine, with the French government paying approximately 72.54 percent, or around €457 million, and Thales Group the remainder.

Source: https://star.worldbank.org/corruption-cases/node/19572.

Reference

StAR and OECD (Stolen Assets Recovery Initiative and Organisation for Economic Co-operation and Development). 2011. *Tracking Anti-Corruption and Asset Recovery Commitments: A Progress Report and Recommendations for Action.* Paris: OECD. http://www.oecd.org.dac/governance-development/49263968.pdf and www .worldbank.org/star.

TABLE 3A.1	Comparative Table of Enforcement on Asset Recovery, 2010–12

| | Assets frozen | | Assets returned | | | | | | | |
| | | | Asset recovery mechanism used | | | | | | | |
Country	No. cases	$ millions	No. cases	$ millions	Criminal confiscation ($ millions)	Criminal restitution, reparations ($ millions)	Non-conviction based confiscation ($ millions)	Private civil action ($ millions)	Other	Resolved by settlement
Australia	0	0	0	0	0	0	0	0	0	0
Austria	No information provided									
Belgium	1	0.3	0	0	0	0	0	0	0	0
Canada	2	2.6	0[a]	0	0	0	0	0	0	0
Chile	No information provided									
Czech Republic	No information provided									
Denmark	0	0	0	0	0	0	0	0	0	0
Estonia	No information provided									
Finland	No information provided									
France	0	0	0	0[b]	0	0	0	0	0	0
Germany	0	0	0	0	0	0	0	0	0	0
Greece	No information provided									
Hungary	No information provided									
Iceland	No information provided									
Ireland	No information provided									
Israel	0[c]		0	0	0	0	0	0	0	
Italy	0	0	0	0	0	0	0	0	0	0[d]
Japan	0	0	0	0	0	0	0	0	0	

Country								
Korea	No information provided							
Luxembourg	7	26.5	0	0	0	0	0	
Mexico	No information provided							
Netherlands	1e	1.2	0	0	0	0	0	
New Zealand	0	0	0	0	0	0	0	
Norway	0	0	0	0	0	0	0	
Poland	No information provided							
Portugal	2	18.4	0	0	0	0	0	
Slovak Republic	0	0	0	0	0	0	0	
Slovenia	No information provided							
Spain	0	0	0	0	0	0	0	
Sweden	0f	0	0	0	0	0	0	
Switzerland	5g	786.1	20.2	19.1	1.1	0	0	1.1
Turkey	No information provided							
United Kingdom	6	451.2h	67.5	0	48.3i	16j	3.1k	51.5
United States	5	112.0	59.5	0	0	0	0	56.6
Total	29	1,398	147.2	19.1	49.4	16	3.1	109.2

Source: Authors' compilation based on responses to StAR/OECD survey.

Notes: a. In the reporting period, Canada imposed one criminal fine under its Corruption of Foreign Public Official Act. A Canada-based company entered a guilty plea in a Calgary court, but given that the case did not result in a return of assets to a foreign jurisdiction, it is not recorded as an "asset recovery."

b. France reported an international commercial arbitration case in which approximately $236 million in fines was paid by a French company, Thales, to Taiwan, China. As an international arbitration outside the scope of UNCAC, it has not been included here. For additional information on the case, see box 3.1.

c. Israel reported five additional criminal cases of assets frozen (to a value of $38.2 million); the cases are not reported here because they were not corruption cases. Israel also reported a domestic investigation and prosecution of corruption involving proceeds of corruption that have been frozen in Panama pursuant to an MLA request ($7.5 million). That case is not considered an asset recovery case for purposes of this study because Israel is the victim state.

d. Italy reported four cases of settlements in bribery cases. Given that the cases did not result in a return of assets to a foreign jurisdiction, they are not recorded as "asset recoveries."

e. In the reporting period, there were five ongoing foreign corruption cases in the Netherlands, most of which were not advanced enough to say anything about criminal assets. The Netherlands reported freezing $4.026 billion of Libyan assets pursuant to UN Security Council resolutions. For purposes of this study, these cases are not included in totals.

f. Sweden reported freezing $1.6 billion of Libyan assets pursuant to UN Security Council resolutions. For purposes of this study, these cases are not included in totals.

g. Switzerland reported freezing $416 million of Libyan assets pursuant to UN Security Council resolutions. For purposes of this study, these cases are not included in totals.

h. The United Kingdom reported having frozen "small amounts" of assets from Tunisia and an unknown amount from Arab Republic of Egypt. It also reported freezing $19.6 billion of Libyan assets pursuant to UN Security Council resolutions. For purposes of this study, the Libyan cases are not included in totals.

i. In addition to the survey response, data in the StAR settlement database include assets returned to Iraq (Weir Group case from 2010; total value $2,375,790).

j. There is also a private civil action filed by the Ukrainian government against a company in the United Kingdom, but no values were provided.

k. In addition to the survey response, data in the StAR settlement database include a voluntary payment to Sub-Saharan African countries (Oxford University Press case from 2012; total value $3,135,220).

4. Policy Developments

Successful asset recovery requires a solid foundation of comprehensive policies and strategies, a legal framework that offers a variety of tools for practitioners, and well-resourced institutions. This chapter discusses country progress in those areas.

Setting Asset Recovery as a Policy Priority

One of the recommendations in the first StAR/OECD report was that countries should implement comprehensive strategic policies to combat corruption and recover assets (StAR and OECD 2011, 13, 35–36). The report found that experiences in Switzerland, the United Kingdom, and the United States had shown that political will—the credible intent of political actors, civil servants, and state actors, most often demonstrated through a well-resourced, high-level country policy or strategy—could generate progress in terms of legislative, institutional, or operational changes, as well as in case results. Those same countries have further developed and improved their policy initiatives over the past two-and-a-half years. In addition, a handful of countries, including Australia, Canada, France, and the Netherlands, have taken steps toward adopting an asset recovery strategy.

Asset recovery policies should have clear objectives, high-level commitment, and sufficient resources (Stephenson et al. 2011, 24–31). The policies should include commitments to improve legislation, institutional capacity, domestic coordination, and international cooperation and to increase the number of cases undertaken and the value of assets frozen or confiscated. They should encourage practitioners to think creatively in overcoming barriers to asset recovery. Reporting measures are important for tracking progress and monitoring results, and so is setting clear benchmarks to encourage proactive initiatives by law enforcement agencies. Box 4.1 describes some examples of good practices that countries have adopted.

Recommendation:

Developed and developing countries should adopt, implement, and fund comprehensive strategic policies to combat corruption and recover assets. Countries should identify gaps and be swift and responsive in addressing obstacles encountered during the asset recovery process. They should evaluate the implementation of their policies and consider changes where needed.

- *Clearly articulated policy.* Switzerland, the United Kingdom, and the United States have all adopted asset recovery as a policy priority and have publicized their commitments through statements and on government websites.

- *High-level buy-in.* Statements supporting asset recovery have been made by the president and attorney general of the United States (U.S. Department of Justice 2012, 2013; U.S. White House 2012), the prime minister and foreign minister of the United Kingdom (U.K. Cabinet Office 2012; 2013; U.K. Foreign and Commonwealth Office 2013; U.K. Home Office 2012), and the president and foreign minister of Switzerland (Switzerland Federal Department of Foreign Affairs 2010; 2011).

- *Resources.* The Netherlands (Afpakken) program for recovery of criminal assets provided additional funding for law enforcement authorities.

- *Commitment to international engagement.* Switzerland launched the Lausanne Process, a global forum that brings practitioners together to discuss pragmatic solutions to asset recovery.

Strengthening International Commitments on Asset Recovery

Several countries have undertaken multilateral efforts to strengthen asset recovery policies, standards, and actions, in particular through the UN Convention against Corruption (UNCAC) Asset Recovery Working Group, the Financial Action Task Force, the G20 Anticorruption Working Group, and the G8 Deauville Partnership (an initiative of the G8 to support countries in the Arab world in democratic transition). In addition to its commitments to improve asset recovery, the G8 Deauville Partnership established the Arab Forum on Asset Recovery (AFAR) to bring together the G8, the countries in transition, and other countries from the Arab region. Through two high-level meetings and three regional trainings, AFAR has provided a forum for regional training and discussion of best practices on cases and effective measures for asset recovery; it has facilitated direct dialogue on cases between countries.

The Financial Action Task Force (FATF) issued new global standards, the revised FATF 40 Recommendations (2012), which strengthened the requirements on customer due diligence, beneficial ownership, politically exposed persons, international cooperation, and responsibility and powers to investigate and prosecute money laundering—all important tools for combating corruption and recovering the proceeds.

As part of these commitments and actions, the G8, the G20, and FATF have also adopted policy, trends analysis, and guidance documents on asset recovery and related topics.

Guidance and Tools on Asset Recovery and Related Topics Produced by G8, G20, and the Financial Action Task Force (FATF)

- **G20, Nine Key Principles of Effective Asset Recovery**, Cannes Summit, France, 2011 (see appendix B). Country profiles have also been drafted and are available on the StAR website.

- **Asset recovery guides**, 2012. Canada, France, Germany, Jersey, Italy, Japan, Switzerland, the United Kingdom, and the United States have published guides on the asset recovery tools and procedures available in each country. They are available at http://star.worldbank.org/star/ArabForum/country-guides-asset-recovery-0.

- **G20, Asset Tracing Country Profiles**, Los Cabos Summit, Mexico 2012. A profile of each G20 country lists the resources available for tracing assets from bank accounts and in the forms of real estate, business and financial interests, and luxury goods. Available at http://g20mexico.org/en/anticorruption and worldbank.org/star.

- **G8 Principles to Prevent the Misuse of Companies and Legal Arrangements**, June 2013. All of the G8 countries have published their national action plans to implement these principles. Available at http://star.worldbank.org/star/about-us/transparency-beneficial-ownership-resource-center.

- **G20 Mutual Legal Assistance Guides of G20 Countries**, Los Cabos Summit, Mexico, 2012. A step-by-step guide to legal requirements for mutual legal assistance in each of the G20 countries. Available at http://g20mexico.org/en/anticorruption.

- **FATF analysis of methods and trends of corruption.** FATF adopted two papers, *Laundering the Proceeds of Corruption* (July 2011), and *Specific Risk Factors in Laundering the Proceeds of Corruption* (FATF 2012). Both are available at http://www.fatf-gafi.org.

- **FATF Best Practice Paper on the Use of the FATF Recommendations to Combat Corruption** (FATF 2013a).

For example, the G20 Anticorruption Working Group adopted *Nine Key Principles of Effective Asset Recovery* and is currently conducting a benchmarking survey against the principles (see appendix B). Some of the country review exercises have been made public and are available on the G20 and StAR websites. Box 4.2 enumerates similar initiatives taken at the international level.

References

FATF (Financial Action Task Force). 2012. *Specific Risk Factors in Laundering the Proceeds of Corruption.* Paris: FATF.

———. 2013. *Best Practice Paper on the Use of the FATF Recommendations to Combat Corruption.* Paris: FATF.

StAR and OECD (Stolen Asset Recovery Initiative and Organisation for Economic Co-operation and Development). 2011. *Tracking Anti-Corruption and Asset Recovery Commitments: A Progress Report and Recommendations for Action.* Paris: OECD.

Stephenson, K. M., L. Gray, R. Power, J. P. Brun, G. Dunker, and M. Panjer. 2011. *Barriers to Asset Recovery: An Analysis of the Key Barriers and Recommendations for Action.* Washington, DC: World Bank.

Switzerland Federal Department of Foreign Affairs. 2010. "Foreign Minister Calmy-Rey Speaks at *No Safe Havens: A Global Forum on Stolen Asset Recovery and Development*," June 8, 2010, Paris.

———. 2011. "Federal President Calmy-Rey at EU-Tunisia Task Force Meeting in Tunis," September 28, 2011, Tunis (accessed November 8, 2013) http://www.swissembassy.org.uk/eda/en/home/recent/media/single.html?id=41409.

United Kingdom Cabinet Office and Prime Minister's Office. 2012. "David Cameron's Address to the United Nations General Assembly," September 26, 2012 (accessed October 26, 2013) https://www.gov.uk/government/speeches/david-camerons-address-to-the-united-nations-general-assembly.

———. 2013. "David Cameron Speaks to the Second Arab Forum on Asset Recovery," October 25, 2013 (accessed November 8, 2013) https://www.gov.uk/government/news/second-arab-forum-on-asset-recovery-marrakesh-26-28-october.

United Kingdom Home Office. 2012. "Written Statement to Parliament: Arab Spring Asset Recovery Task Force," December 17, 2012, London (accessed October 26, 2013) https://www.gov.uk/government/speeches/arab-spring-asset-recovery-task-force.

United States Department of Justice. 2012. "Attorney General Eric Holder Speaks at the Arab Forum on Asset Recovery," Doha, Qatar, September 13, 2012 (accessed October 26, 2013) http://www.justice.gov/iso/opa/ag/speeches/2012/ag-speech-120913.html.

———. 2013. "Attorney General Eric Holder Delivers Remarks at the Arab Forum on Asset Recovery," Marrakesh, Morocco, October 28, 2013 (accessed November 8, 2013) http://www.justice.gov/iso/opa/ag/speeches/2013/ag-speech-131028.html.

United States White House. 2012. "President Obama's Message to the Arab Forum on Asset Recovery," September 12, 2012 (accessed November 8, 2013) http://www.whitehouse.gov/photos-and-video/video/2012/09/10/president-obama-s-message-arab-forum-asset-recovery.

5. Legislative Developments

The responses to the StAR/OECD questionnaire show that many OECD members are expanding their legal tools and powers. Fourteen of the 20 responding countries reported having introduced new laws to facilitate asset recovery between January 2010 and June 2012. Table 5.1 shows a snapshot of OECD country progress on a selection of asset recovery laws that experts have identified as important (Stephenson et al. 2011; Brun et al. 2011; G8 asset recovery principles, see box 4.2). The list of asset recovery laws is not exhaustive, however, nor does the fact that a particular country has a law mean that it is working effectively.

Some of the new laws codified one or more of the tools in the UN Convention against Corruption (UNCAC). Of note, Ireland and the Czech Republic have now ratified the convention, leaving Germany, Japan, and New Zealand the only OECD members that are not yet states parties to the UNCAC.

Recommendation:

Germany, Japan, and New Zealand should ratify the UNCAC.

Other countries have passed laws to fill gaps or loopholes identified in existing legislation. For example, the United States passed the Preserving Foreign Criminal Assets for Forfeiture Act of 2010, to permit the freezing of foreign assets before or after the initiation of proceedings in the foreign jurisdiction. This action followed a U.S. court decision that interpreted the earlier law in this area as requiring a final forfeiture order for any freezing of foreign assets—an interpretation that would have severely impaired asset recovery efforts by allowing defendants additional time to move assets.

Most interesting, however, is that many of the laws have introduced innovative mechanisms for overcoming obstacles commonly encountered in asset recovery cases, such as proving the link between the asset and the offense, the requirement for a criminal conviction, or the need for some degree of international cooperation from the foreign jurisdiction. Some examples of these laws and their use by OECD members are outlined below.

Rebuttable Presumptions

Rebuttable presumptions help the prosecution (or plaintiff) meet the burden of proof. The prosecution establishes a defined set of circumstances sufficient to raise a

TABLE 5.1 Asset Recovery Legal Framework in OECD Member Countries

	Ratified or acceded to UNCAC	New asset recovery laws	Rapid freezing (48 hours)	Direct enforcement of foreign confiscation orders	Non-conviction based confiscation law	Recognize foreign non-conviction based confiscation orders	Foreign countries can initiate civil action in domestic courts	Courts can order compensation, restitution, or other damages to a foreign jurisdiction
Australia	Yes	Yes[a]	Yes	Yes	Yes	Yes	No	No
Belgium	Yes	EU only[b]	Yes[c]	EU only	No	EU only	Yes	
Canada	Yes	Yes[d]	Yes[e]	Yes	Yes[f]	Yes[g]	Yes	Yes
Denmark	Yes	No	Yes	EU only	No	No	Yes[h]	Yes
France	Yes	Yes[i]	No	No	No	Yes	Yes	Yes
Germany	No	EU only[j]	Yes[k]	No	No	No	Yes[l]	Yes
Israel	Yes	Yes[m]	No[n]	Yes	Yes	Yes	Yes	Yes
Italy	Yes	Yes[o]	No	Yes	Yes	Yes	Yes	Yes
Japan	No	No	No	Yes	No	No	Yes	No
Luxembourg	Yes	No	Yes	No	No	No	No	Yes
Netherlands	Yes	Yes[p]	Yes[q]	EU only	No	No	Yes	
New Zealand	No	No	No	Yes	Yes		No	Yes
Norway	Yes	No	Yes	Yes	No	Yes	Yes	Yes
Portugal	Yes	Yes[r]	Yes[s]	Yes	Yes	Yes	Yes	Yes[t]

Slovak Republic	Yes	Yes	Yes	Yes	Yes	Yes	Yes
Spain	Yes	EU only[u]	EU only	No	No	Yes	Yes
Sweden	Yes	EU only[v]	EU only	Limited[w]	No	Yes	Yes
Switzerland	Yes	-Yes[x]	Yes	Yes	Yes	Yes	Yes
United Kingdom	Yes	No	No	Yes[y]	Yes	Yes	Yes
United States	Yes	Yes[z]	No	No	Yes	Yes	Yes

Source: Authors' compilation based on responses to StAR/OECD survey.

Notes: Responses were not received from Austria, Chile, Czech Republic, Estonia, Finland, Greece, Hungary, Iceland, Ireland, Korea Rep., Mexico, Poland, Slovenia, and Turkey.

a. In 2010, Australia introduced "unexplained wealth" into the Proceeds of Crime Act 2002.

b. Law of 26 November 2011 and Law of 19 March 2012 (Moniteur Belge 04 April 2012) facilitate mutual recognition of court orders in criminal cases between member states of the European Union.

c. Belgian Financial Investigation Unit can freeze assets up to five days following a request by a foreign jurisdiction.

d. In 2011, Canada passed the Freezing Assets of Corrupt Foreign Official Act and Freezing Assets of Corrupt Foreign Officials (Tunisia and Egypt, Arab Rep.). Regulations.

e. Yes, in accordance with conditions of the Freezing Assets of Corrupt Foreign Officials Act.

f. Non-conviction based confiscation can only be pursued at the state level, not at the federal level, in Canada. Eight Canadian provinces have laws that allow for civil forfeiture: British Columbia, Alberta, Saskatchewan, Manitoba, Quebec, New Brunswick, and Nova Scotia.

g. Non-conviction based orders can only be recognized at the provincial level in accordance with the provincial laws.

h. Administration of Justice Act.

i. Law 768 of 9 July 2010 and Law 409 of 27 March 2012.

j. Legislation simplifying exchange of information and intelligence between EU member states.

k. Prosecutors and/or law enforcement officials can freeze without judicial authorization. See also Section 67, paragraphs 3 and 4, of the Act on International Cooperation in Criminal Matters.

l. Section 32 of the German Civil Procedure Law.

m. The Legal Assistance Law was amended in October 2010 (Amendment No. 7), authorizing the minister of justice to exempt requesting jurisdictions from providing undertakings.

n. Current legislation requires a judicial order to freeze assets. Upcoming legislative amendments will enable the government to freeze assets swiftly upon foreign request (Amendment No. 7).

o. Law 190 of November 6, 2012. The law brings a comprehensive set of measures to prevent and combat corruption; it also contains provisions aimed at facilitating asset recovery.

p. Law expanding the possibilities for confiscation of illegally obtained advantages (2011). The law also introduced new provisions related to the need to show the origin of obtained advantages.

q. Assets can be frozen within 24 hours if the foreign order or the request is from an EU member state. Outside the EU, urgent cases can be sent directly to a magistrate.

r. Law 45/2011, June 24, 2011, creating the National Asset Recovery Office.

s. Legal framework allows freeze of assets within hours based on a request made directly to the Public Prosecution Service–DCIAP (Central Department for Criminal Investigation and Prosecution).

t. Law 144/99 of August 31, 1999.

u. Act 4/2010 implementing the EU Council Framework Decision 2006/783/JHA; Act 5/2010 amending the Criminal Procedure Code to regulate the ARO and amending the criminal code to include extended confiscation, implementing EU Framework Decision 2005/212/JHA.

v. Law 423 of 2011 applying EU Council Decision 2006/783/JHA.

w. Non-conviction based confiscation is allowed if a sanction can no longer be imposed, for example, because of the death of the offender (chapter 36, section 14 of the Criminal Code), and the proceeds or instrumentalities of crime can be confiscated under limited circumstances (chapter 36 of the Criminal Code). Confiscation without a connection to a criminal conviction is generally not allowed.

x. Switzerland Federal Act of October 1, 2010, Restitution of Assets Illicitly Obtained by Politically Exposed Persons and Restitution of Illicit Assets Act (RIAA), came into effect on February 1, 2011.

y. Proceeds of Crime Act 2002, sections 444 and 447.

z. Preserving Foreign Criminal Assets for Forfeiture Act of 2010, Pub. L. No. 111-342, 124 Stat. 3607 (codified as amended at 28 U.S.C. § 2467(d)(3)(A)(i) (2012)).

presumption, and the party against whom the presumption exists has the burden to overcome it by presenting proof (that is, the burden of proof is reversed). If the party fails, the presumption is converted into a fact. Switzerland's Restitution of Illicit Assets Act, adopted in 2011, provides for a presumption of the illicit nature of the assets in cases in which the enrichment of the politically exposed person (PEP) is clearly exorbitant and the degree of corruption of the state or of the person in question is notoriously great (see box 5.1). Where successful, such presumptions allow for the freezing, forfeiture, and restitution of the proceeds of corruption in cases of failed states where mutual legal assistance (MLA) requests cannot succeed.

Other rebuttable presumptions, such as extended confiscation and criminal lifestyle presumptions, are activated upon conviction for an offense, raising an inference of the illicit nature of all assets (or benefits). To rebut the presumption, the defendant must prove the assets were lawfully acquired; otherwise the court can accept as a fact that the benefits derived over an extended period are benefits of the offense (in extended confiscation) or the assets are the proceeds of crime. This allows for confiscation of assets that may have been derived from other offenses for which the individual was not charged or convicted. Extended confiscation has been adopted in France, Germany, Norway, and Sweden; criminal lifestyle presumptions are available in the United Kingdom.

BOX 5.1   Good Practice: Innovative Legislation to Overcome Barriers

In 2011, Switzerland passed the act Federal Restitution of Illicit Assets of Politically Exposed Persons Obtained by Unlawful Means, to overcome a number of barriers that had emerged in high-profile cases (e.g., Mobutu, Duvalier). It governs the freezing, forfeiture, and restitution of the assets of politically exposed persons (PEPs) and their close associates in cases where a request for mutual assistance in criminal matters cannot succeed because of the failure of the judicial system in the requesting state. There is no need for a conviction of the PEP in his or her jurisdiction of origin, and the law provides for a presumption of the illicit nature of assets in cases where the enrichment of the PEP is clearly exorbitant and the degree of corruption of the state or the person in question is notoriously great.

Recently Switzerland proposed a new law on the freezing and restitution of potentates' assets, the Act on the Restitution of Illicit Assets. The draft law aims to regulate all matters relating to the freezing, confiscation, and restitution illicit assets linked to foreign dictators. It proposes an extension of the possibility of administrative confiscation. It further contains provisions on targeted measures, enabling the Swiss government to support a requesting country in its efforts to obtain the restitution of assets of criminal origin transferred abroad. The parliamentary debate was pending at the time this report was written.

Source: Authors' compilation based on Federal Act on the Restitution of Assets of Politically Exposed Persons obtained by Unlawful Means, available at http://www.eda.admin.ch/etc/medialib/downloads/edazen/topics/finec/intcr.Par.0024.File.tmp/LRAI_en.pdf; and "Illicit Assets of Politically Exposed Persons (PEPs)," http://www.eda.admin.ch/eda/en/home/topics/finec/poexp.html.

Although extended confiscation and criminal lifestyle presumptions are more often used for drug and organized crime cases, countries should apply these presumptions in corruption cases. Switzerland has accomplished this in an innovative case against General Sani Abacha and his family, in which members of the Abacha family and close associates were qualified as a criminal organization. This provision allowed for the reversal of the burden of proof, requiring the wrongdoers to prove that they had acquired their assets legitimately.

Administrative Freezing and Confiscation Measures

Other innovative measures that were quite successful—in terms both of broad application and of actual results obtained—were the laws, decisions, and decrees passed requiring the freezing of assets held by individuals suspected of misappropriating assets of Arab Republic of Egypt, Libya, or Tunisia. Canada, the European Union, Switzerland, and the United States are among the countries that acted rapidly to freeze assets, ultimately freezing 39 percent of the total value of assets frozen between 2010 and June 2012.

These measures differed from past cases because they were administrative in nature—an order by government to banks and other entities to freeze assets—as opposed to requiring a judicial order by a court or investigating magistrate, as well as a mutual legal assistance request. Such measures are typically reserved for situations such as political upheaval or internal turmoil in the foreign jurisdiction, their purpose being to preserve assets and prevent them from being transferred elsewhere. They are not meant to replace or circumvent mutual legal assistance. MLA will be required at some point, when domestic law enforcement needs evidence from the foreign jurisdiction to prove money laundering or support foreign bribery cases, or when the foreign jurisdiction needs to enforce its final judgment in domestic courts.

However, MLA is known to be slow, formalistic, and complicated even for experienced jurisdictions, and more so for developing jurisdictions or those in transition. The added risk of dissipation or movement of assets militates in favor of taking proactive steps to freeze assets administratively and allow time for the jurisdiction harmed by corruption to respond. In this way, administrative orders and similar measures can freeze assets prior to a full formal request, complementing the MLA process.

As a result of the progress achieved by laws in Canada and Switzerland, the United Kingdom announced that it is considering adoption of similar administrative measures (United Kingdom Foreign and Commonwealth Office 2013). Switzerland has proposed a new law expanding these administrative measures to cover the eventual confiscation of assets (see box 5.2).

Once these freezes are in place, several barriers have been encountered that have hindered progress in the actual recovery of the assets. The requesting jurisdictions indicate that they are unaware of the assets that are frozen and are having difficulty providing

In the wake of the Arab Spring, several OECD members implemented administrative freezes pursuant to domestic laws or regional decisions. It was the first time that such administrative freezes were adopted and implemented so widely.

For example, **Canada** adopted the Freezing Assets of Corrupt Foreign Officials Act and the Freezing Assets of Corrupt Foreign Officials (Tunisia and Egypt) Regulations, requiring banks, companies, and other entities to freeze the assets of named individuals. The legislation does not address confiscation of the assets or asset return.

The European Union adopted EU Council Decision 2011/72/CFSP (January 31, 2011) and EU Council Decision 2011/172/CFSP (March 21, 2011), directing member states to freeze the assets of persons responsible for misappropriation of Arab Republic of Egypt and Tunisian state funds and directing member states on conditions for release.

Switzerland issued ordinances requiring banks to identify and freeze the assets of targeted individuals suspected of misappropriation in Tunisia (January 19, 2011), Arab Republic of Egypt (February 2, 2011), and Libya (February 21, 2011).

The United States issued executive order 13566 to block assets related to Libya (February 25, 2011).

United Nations Security Council Resolutions 1970 (2011) and 1973 (2011) imposed an asset freeze against Gaddafi and his family members, as well as all funds, financial assets, and economic resources owned or controlled by the Libyan authorities (e.g., Central Bank of Libya, the Libyan Investment Authority, and the Libyan National Oil Corporation). Although some of these cases may have involved the proceeds of corruption, it is impossible to distinguish them for purposes of this report.

the information or evidence necessary to keep the freeze in place. Many of their initial requests are returned with requests for additional information—a frustrating yet frequent occurrence in the MLA process for all jurisdictions. Political instability and the continuing transition process have slowed progress even further, particularly in Arab Republic of Egypt and Libya.

Some requested jurisdictions have taken steps to support foreign practitioners and information sharing. Some have used spontaneous disclosures to provide information on assets frozen (consistent with Articles 46(4) and 56 of UNCAC); others have taken steps to build the capacity of practitioners in the foreign jurisdictions through placement of regional advisers and mentors (see also chapter 6). The United Kingdom pushed for changes to allow better information sharing between EU member states and Arab Spring countries, resulting in a proposed European Commission directive (European Commission 2012).

Unexplained Wealth Provisions, Illicit or Unjust Enrichment Laws

Australia introduced new laws permitting the confiscation of "unexplained wealth" in circumstances where a person's total wealth exceeds the value of their wealth that was lawfully acquired (Australia Proceeds of Crime Act 2002, section 179E). If the defendant cannot prove that their wealth is lawful, the court may order confiscation of the assets. These laws have been focused on drug offenses, but nothing precludes their application in corruption offenses.

Non-conviction Based Confiscation

Confiscation in the absence of a conviction (NCB confiscation) continues to be an effective mechanism for freezing and confiscating assets. Between January 2010 and June 2012, almost $60 million of $146.2 million in proceeds returned were captured pursuant to NCB confiscation actions. Despite these successful asset recovery cases however, most OECD members have yet to adopt laws permitting the confiscation of assets in the absence of a conviction.

Fortunately, there have been improvements in regional cooperation on NCB cases: Countries of the European Union permit EU-to-EU country cooperation on these cases, as well as enforcement of foreign NCB confiscation orders, even in the absence of domestic NCB confiscation laws. The application of this principle by more countries and at the international level has been encouraged in an Interpretive Note to revised FATF Recommendation 38.

Legislative Gaps Remain

Although progress has been made in some countries, others do not have the tools or powers that have been applied in successful asset recovery cases. Laws permitting rapid freezing of assets, NCB confiscation, and direct enforcement of foreign confiscation orders are particularly lacking. Even when countries have the tools, they may not be applied equally to all foreign jurisdictions. For example, some European Union jurisdictions have confiscation laws that do not apply to jurisdictions outside the European Union.

Another area for further development is asset tracing. The G20 countries recently produced country profiles showing the resources or measures available to trace assets in the form of bank accounts, real estate, business and financial interests, and luxury goods (G20 Countries 2012). The gaps in resources available are significant and critical to address, especially as research shows wide misuse of corporate vehicles in big corruption cases (Van der Does et al. 2011, 21).

Recommendation:

To be effective in asset recovery, OECD member states should develop laws and regulations adequate for accomplishing the following:

- Rapidly freeze assets, including in the absence of an MLA request.

- Confiscate assets in the absence of a conviction (NCB confiscation).

- Permit direct enforcement of foreign criminal or NCB orders and cooperation with other countries on NCB cases.

- Require service providers to collect beneficial ownership information and allow access to it.

- Permit spontaneous disclosures and other means to share information on a freeze with the foreign jurisdiction involved.

- Help practitioners overcome barriers to asset recovery (for example, enact laws introducing legal presumptions, unexplained wealth or illicit enrichment provisions, extended confiscation, confiscation of equivalent value).

Including Asset Return in Settlement Agreements

Another area requiring greater attention is how to bring about more asset returns in the context of settlement agreements. *Left Out of the Bargain,* a recent StAR study on settlement agreements in foreign bribery cases and their implications for asset recovery, broadly defines a "settlement" as any procedure short of a full trial, encompassing civil and administrative, as well as criminal mechanisms (Oduor et al. 2013, 8, 17–20). Such agreements are undertaken in both common law and civil law countries and in developed and developing countries.

The main conclusion of the study by Oduor et al. (2013, 2) is that significant monetary sanctions have been imposed in settlement cases, with hardly any of the assets in question being returned to the jurisdictions whose officials have allegedly been bribed. The data gathered by the StAR/OECD survey and the StAR Settlements Cases database support that conclusion and parallel what Oduor and coauthors found in their study, which covered 1999 through mid-2012.[1]

---

1. *Left Out of the Bargain* looked at 395 settlement cases between 1999 and mid-2012 and found that only 3.3 percent had been returned or ordered returned to the countries whose officials were bribed or allegedly bribed. Parallel and separate research for this report should that in 120 settlements. In 120 settlements in foreign bribery cases between 2010 and June 2012, approximately $3.4 billion in reparations, restitution, fines, disgorgement of profits, and the like, was ordered, according to the StAR Settlements database (http ://www.worldbank.org/star). Yet only $109.2 million, or 3.2 percent, has been returned or ordered returned by OECD members to countries whose officials were bribed or allegedly bribed.

There is certainly room for more consideration of settlements as an option for asset returns. It is encouraging to observe that 74 percent of the assets returned during the period that this report covers followed a settlement agreement (see figure 3.10, in chapter 3, for a summary). Also deserving discussion is the impact of settlements on pending and future cases in other jurisdictions, as discussed in *Left Out of the Bargain* (Oduor et al. 2013, 57). Concern exists, first, that the principle of double jeopardy could mean that the settlement of a case in one jurisdiction could prevent subsequent prosecutions of the same case in another jurisdiction. There is also a practical concern that the law enforcement and judicial authorities of a country that has reached a settlement might be reluctant to provide mutual legal assistance.

Recommendation:

Countries should engage in a domestic or international policy debate on how asset returns can be incorporated into settlement agreements in corruption cases and should consider legislative changes necessary to permit the inclusion of third parties in settlement agreements in foreign bribery cases.

References

European Commission. 2012. "Directive of the European Parliament and of the Council on the Freezing and Confiscation of Proceeds of Crime in the EU." Brussels: European Commission.

G20 Countries Anticorruption Working Group. 2012. *G20 Asset Tracing Country Profiles*, Los Cabos Summit, Los Cabos, Mexico.

Oduor, J., F. M. U. Fernando, A. Flah, D. Gottwald, J. M. Hauch, M. Mathias, J. W. Park, and O. Stolpe. 2013. *Left Out of the Bargain: Settlements in Foreign Bribery Cases and Implications for Asset Recovery*. Washington, DC: World Bank.

Stephenson, K. M., L. Gray, R. Power, J. P. Brun, G. Dunker, and M. Panjer. 2011. *Barriers to Asset Recovery: An Analysis of the Key Barriers and Recommendations for Action*. Washington, DC: World Bank.

United Kingdom Foreign and Commonwealth Office. 2013. "Opening Statement by Mr. Dominic Grieve, Attorney General of the United Kingdom," Arab Forum on Asset Recovery, Marrakesh, Morocco (accessed November 8, 2013) https://www.gov.uk/government/news/second-arab-forum-on-asset-recovery-marrakesh-26-28-october.

Van der Does de Willebois, E., E. M. Halter, R. A. Harrison, J. W. Park, and J. C. Sharman. 2011. *The Puppet Masters: How the Corrupt Use Legal Structures to Hide Stolen Assets and What to Do about It*. Washington, DC: World Bank.

6. Institutional Developments

OECD members continue to make institutional changes to recover the proceeds of corruption.

Specialized Units That Focus on Asset Recovery

Four countries—Canada, Spain, Sweden, and the United States—have joined the United Kingdom in establishing special units that focus exclusively on corruption offenses and recovery of corruption proceeds (see box 6.1). The United Kingdom expanded its approach slightly to create a cross-government task force.

Other OECD members have established specialized units that focus on recovery of the proceeds of all crimes, including corruption. Most recently Portugal joined other countries of the European Union in establishing an asset recovery office, and Australia established the Criminal Asset Confiscation Taskforce in 2011. Steps have also been taken to identify and address challenges: A recent evaluation by the European Commission cited lack of authority to access bank information, absence of a secure platform for exchange of information, and other resource problems. The EU is undertaking steps to amend the legal framework to overcome these challenges (European Commission 2010; 2011).

Adequate Resources and a Mandate and Incentives to be Proactive in Asset Recovery

Whatever modality countries select, it is important that their agencies have a clear mandate and sufficient powers and resources, and that they are adequately staffed with personnel who specialize in asset recovery cases and have expertise in financial investigation, forensic accounting, and conducting cases. Also critical are incentives to make foreign corruption cases a high priority and pursue them proactively. The data show that domestic prosecution of cases of foreign bribery or money laundering is an important avenue for freezing and returning assets. Such cases are initiated following suspicious transaction reports, media reports, information from whistleblowers, or other triggers—not pursuant to an MLA request. As with administrative freezes, proactive investigations and prosecutions may be the only way to prevent the dissipation and movement of assets. Cases will eventually require mutual legal assistance requests from (or to) the foreign jurisdiction, and so it is important to alert the foreign jurisdiction of the investigation through a spontaneous disclosure and open the channels of cooperation as soon as possible.

Forming and Using Practitioner Networks

Many OECD members continue to develop contacts and share information through practitioner networks as a way to foster trust and international cooperation. Such networks have expanded opportunities for informal assistance, outside the realm of a formal mutual legal assistance request, and that is an important first step in international cooperation (Brun et al. 2011, 121–37). Almost all OECD members have appointed focal points under the Global Focal Point Network supported by StAR and Interpol. The initiative has brought together a network of practitioners representing 99 jurisdictions; only Belgium, Iceland, Ireland, Italy, Japan, and Sweden are missing focal points. Other regional networks have also been helpful on recovery of proceeds of corruption, such as Eurojust, a network of national prosecutors, magistrates, and police officers fighting against serious organized crime, and the Camden Asset Recovery Inter-Agency Network (CARIN), a network of law enforcement and judicial experts on confiscation and asset recovery in mostly EU countries. There are also other CARIN-style regional networks, including the Asset Recovery Agency for Southern Africa (ARINSA), Asset

Recovery Agency for Eastern Africa (ARIN-EA), Asset Recovery Agency for Asia Pacific (ARIN-AP), and the Asset Recovery Network of GAFISUD (RRAG).

Capacity Building in Developing Countries

Asset recovery cases generally require investigations in both the requested and requesting countries. Intelligence, information, and evidence need to be gathered, assets must be traced and frozen, and cases pursued. International cooperation is undertaken to share evidence in support of a foreign case or to enforce a domestic order. Requesting jurisdictions often struggle with asset tracing and financial investigations, understanding requests from foreign jurisdictions, and gathering the needed evidence. Where needed, some OECD members have broadened their asset recovery efforts to include the development of institutions and practitioners beyond their borders.

Such capacity building is envisioned under the fundamental principle of shared responsibility in UNCAC. According to a recent publication, "The area where the most work remains is in the capacity building of developing countries to undertake asset recovery efforts both within and beyond their borders" (Vlassis, Gottwald, and Park 2013, 171). Capacity development is also a priority of the Accra Agenda for Action.

Some of the programs offered by requested jurisdictions and international organizations include secondments; hosting case conferences; training programs for financial intelligence analysts, investigators, prosecutors, and judges; and placement of in-country mentors, resident legal advisers or liaison magistrates (see box 6.2

| BOX 6.2 | Good Practices in Building Capacity of Requesting Jurisdictions |

- **Regional advisers and liaison magistrates.** The United Kingdom has posted a crown prosecutor and a regional asset recovery adviser to provide direct assistance in drafting mutual legal assistance requests and help in the asset recovery process. France and the United States have also posted regional advisers or liaison magistrates.

- **Day-to-day mentors.** StAR has provided client countries with local mentors. The mentor provides day-to-day advice, training, or support to practitioners working on cases and assists with building long-term capacity. The mentor's job is to support practitioners, not to substitute for them.

- **Occasional mentors.** In May 2012 the United States appointed two Department of Justice attorneys specialized in the recovery of illicitly acquired assets to work exclusively with counterparts in Middle East and North African transition countries, as part of its support for the Deauville Partnership with Arab countries in transition and the Asset Recovery Action Plan.

- **Study tours and training for those working on cases.** StAR and several OECD members have conducted training in developing countries. Such training is an opportunity for both parties to discuss their legal frameworks ideas for pursuing cases through bilateral meetings.

for examples). Anecdotal evidence suggests that such efforts have helped developing countries to prioritize and initiate their own investigations and build trust with foreign counterparts, as well as to generate information and evidence (or a court order) that supports an ongoing asset recovery case.

Recommendation:

The following steps are recommended to OECD members:

- Establish and adequately resource specialized teams or units to work on asset recovery cases. Such teams must be staffed with personnel who specialize in asset recovery cases, with expertise in financial investigation and forensic accounting, and with attorneys experienced in asset recovery.

- Establish incentives for domestic law enforcement to initiate investigations into cases of money laundering or foreign bribery.

- Engage in and use practitioner networks.

- Conduct capacity building in developing countries to support effective investigations, international cooperation, and the sharing of good practices.

References

European Commission. 2010. "Communication from the Commission to the European Parliament and the Council: The EU Internal Strategy in Action: Five Steps Towards a More Secure Europe." COM (2010) 673 of 22.11.2010. Brussels: European Commission.
———. 2011. "Report from the Commission to the European Parliament and to the Council Based on Article 8 of the Council Decision 2007/845/JHA of 6 December 2007 Concerning Cooperation between Asset Recovery Offices of the Member States in the Field of Tracing and Identification of Proceeds from, or Other Property Related to, Crime." 12.4.2011. Brussels: European Commission.
Vlassis, D., D. Gottwald, and J. W. Park. 2013. "Chapter V of UNCAC: Five Years on Experiences, Obstacles and Reforms on Asset Recovery." In *Emerging Trends in Asset Recovery*, edited by G. F. Zinkemagel, C. Monteith, and P. Gomes Pereira. Bern: Peter Lang AG, International Academic Publishers.

7. The Role of Developing Countries

In the Accra Agenda for Action, developing countries committed themselves to "improving systems of investigation, legal redress, accountability and transparency in the use of public funds" (para. 24(d)). As partner countries in the Busan partnership, they share the same commitment as the donor countries to "national and international policies, legal frameworks and institutional arrangements for the tracing, freezing and recovery of illegal assets" (para. 33(b)).

Successful asset recovery requires commitment and action by all jurisdictions, especially the jurisdiction of the corrupt official. Allegations of corruption and a list of assets held by the person in question are not sufficient on their own to entitle a country to the assets. That the assets are illegal must be established, and in most cases, the country of the corrupt official is best placed to provide the necessary information, evidence, or judicial order that will allow the financial center to freeze, confiscate, and return them.

A detailed review of progress that the developing countries have made is outside the scope of this report. However, the findings of the recent StAR report *Left Out of the Bargain* (Oduor et al. 2013) provide helpful insight into their activity in one type of corruption offense, foreign bribery. That report found that very few jurisdictions have taken enforcement action against foreign companies or individuals who have bribed their public officials. Of 395 cases, most were prosecuted by developed jurisdictions. Among the developing countries, only Nigeria, Costa Rica, and Lesotho have concluded cases (Oduor et al. 2013, 53). Although cases may have occurred in which the jurisdiction was not aware of a bribe, in many cases jurisdictions simply took no action, in spite of preliminary evidence of criminal activity.

For the developing countries to change that, the following are important conditions:

- **Political will.** Commitment to recover assets must start at the highest levels, backed by necessary resources, legislative and institutional changes, and determination to increase domestic coordination and international cooperation.
- **Effective laws and institutions.** A strong legislative and regulatory framework—with multiple legal tools to detect criminal activity and illicit financial flows, rapidly freeze assets, and conduct effective investigations and court processes—is necessary. Non-conviction based confiscation laws deserve particular consideration. They have been particularly effective in asset recovery in cases of the death, flight, or immunity of the corrupt official but are yet to be widely adopted. Effective institutions with operational independence are critical, in particular for financial intelligence units and anticorruption authorities.
- **Investigations and pursuit of cases.** Such concrete action is critical. It signals that the jurisdiction is serious about fighting corruption and recovering assets, a message that is important for deterrence and to build credibility with foreign counterparts.

Even when a foreign jurisdiction is taking the lead in pursuing a case, investigations will be necessary to prove the illicit nature of the proceeds being pursued (box 7.1).

- **Domestic coordination as an essential foundation.** Effective interaction among agencies will facilitate strategic thinking, setting priorities among cases, and determining the best option for asset recovery. Because of the complexity of asset recovery cases, a high-level commitment to engage all domestic stakeholders (including the financial intelligence unit) in the effort to recover stolen assets is needed.

- **Informal practitioner-to-practitioner cooperation.** Such cooperation is a critical step in international cooperation. For the purposes of this report, "informal cooperation" includes any type of assistance that does not require a formal MLA request. Such informal cooperation is often outlined in MLA legislation and may involve formal authorities, agencies, or administrations. Many practitioners immediately resort to drafting an MLA request when they determine that international cooperation is required. However, important information can be obtained more quickly and with fewer formalities through direct communication between domestic agencies and their foreign counterparts (e.g., financial intelligence units, law enforcement authorities, prosecutors, and investigating magistrates). Even information that is common knowledge, or easily obtainable in one jurisdiction, can be extremely useful to the foreign counterpart. Such cooperation can help those operatives build a case, trace and freeze assets, build trust between counterparts, and strategize and prioritize on cases, as well as provide a proper foundation for an MLA request. Practitioner networks, such as the

---

| BOX 7.1 | Good Practices—Cooperation between Requested and Requesting Jurisdictions; Actions by Developing Countries |

Cooperation between Requested and Requesting Jurisdictions

Authorities in Nigeria and the United Kingdom have maintained an ongoing relationship in the corruption cases of three state governors, Diepreye Alamieyeseigha, Joshua Dariye, and James Ibori. Nigeria's Economic and Financial Crimes Commission and the London Metropolitan Police Proceeds of Corruption Unit have collaborated on the seizure, confiscation, and ultimate return of proceeds of corruption. A range of asset recovery avenues were pursued, including a corruption case in Nigeria, a money-laundering case in the United Kingdom, non-conviction based asset confiscation in the United Kingdom, and civil actions.

Actions by Developing Countries

In the Bonny Island LNG case, Nigerian government officials were bribed by several foreign companies involved in a liquefied natural gas project. The Nigerian government has prosecuted several foreign companies for paying bribes to a range of Nigerian government officials. As part of the settlement agreement, international corporations and consortia have agreed to pay compensation to the Nigerian government. Similar actions have been taken by other governments such as Costa Rica and Greece.

Source: Oduor et al. 2013, 53.

Egmont Group and the Global Focal Point Network (StAR/Interpol), can be sources for informal contacts.

- **Development of the capacity of practitioners.** Jurisdictions need to develop the technical capacity of those conducting the day-to-day activities—the financial analysts, investigators, prosecutors, and judges. Developing countries should reach out to development agencies, international organizations, the StAR Initiative, and other technical assistance providers to find out about technical assistance that is available (see also chapter 4, under the subhead "Institutional Developments," for some programs that requested jurisdictions are conducting). To support learning, StAR has developed a series of practical handbooks and policy notes on asset recovery issues (see box 7.2).

Recommendation:

Developing countries should increase their efforts to combat corruption and recover assets by taking the following steps:

- Obtain high-level political commitment to asset recovery, as well as the commitment and involvement of the various domestic stakeholders.

- Adopt and implement necessary legislative and institutional changes, in particular NCB confiscation and mechanisms to rapidly freeze assets.

- Conduct cases and investigations.

- Engage in international cooperation using both informal practitioner-to-practitioner channels and formal mutual legal assistance.

- Develop domestic capacity to conduct cases, reaching out to development agencies and international organizations where required.

BOX 7.2	StAR's Practical Handbooks and Policy Notes on Asset Recovery (Available at http://www.worldbank.org/star)

- *Asset Recovery Handbook*
- *Barriers to Asset Recovery*
- *Non-Conviction Based Asset Forfeiture Guide*
- *The Puppet Masters: How the Corrupt Use Legal Structures to Hide Stolen Assets and What to Do about It*
- *Left Out of the Bargain: Settlements in Foreign Bribery Cases and Implications for Asset Recovery*
- *Quantification of the Proceeds of Bribery*
- *On the Take: Criminalizing Illicit Enrichment to Fight Corruption*
- *Public Office, Private Interests: Accountability through Asset and Income Disclosures*
- *Management of Returned Assets*
- *Politically Exposed Persons: Preventive Measures for the Banking Sector*

Reference

Oduor, J., F. M. U. Fernando, A. Flah, D. Gottwald, J. M. Hauch, M. Mathias, J. W. Park, and O. Stolpe. 2013. *Left Out of the Bargain: Settlements in Foreign Bribery Cases and Implications for Asset Recovery.* Washington, DC: World Bank.

8. The Role of Development Agencies

The recovery of the proceeds of corruption has the potential for a significant development impact. First, recovery of a fraction of the estimated billions that are stolen annually from developing countries would provide much-needed funding for development programs. Second, depriving corrupt officials of their ill-gotten gains provides a powerful deterrent to criminal outflows. Finally, the implementation of policy, legislative, and institutional reforms to prevent corruption and advance asset recovery can result in long-lasting reforms and improved credibility of governance.

What part development agencies play will vary depending on the domestic context and their mandate and role in formulating broader government policy. However, the Accra and Busan commitments represent an opportunity for OECD members to expand development assistance beyond the traditional field of good governance, improved accountability, and corruption prevention programs to activities that focus on the criminal justice side of the corruption issue. Whatever role is selected, all agencies will need to consider innovative ways to support their countries' efforts to move the stolen asset recovery agenda forward.

That focus needs to encompass planning and advocacy activities in both developing and developed countries. Technical assistance can be provided to developing countries to support their capacities to prevent corruption, conduct financial crime investigations, develop legislation, and request international assistance. Domestically, development agencies can be instrumental in supporting the necessary policy, legislative, and institutional changes in their respective countries and the capacity of domestic investigators to conduct financial crime investigations. Examples of possible areas for action are outlined below.

Incorporating Asset Recovery Efforts into Development Policies

As discussed above, political will—the credible intent of the various stakeholders—is critical to successful asset recovery. Development agencies must make asset recovery a priority in their strategic planning and push other stakeholders to do the same. Understanding the impact of corruption on developing economies, as well as the potential development impact of asset recovery, can illuminate the importance of these issues. For example, in 2011 the World Bank conducted a study on the development impact of money laundering on the economies of Malawi and Namibia. The report estimated that the loss of revenues linked to corruption and tax evasion amounts to 5 percent to 10 percent of GDP.

More recently, the G20 Anticorruption Working Group initiated a study reviewing the impact of corruption on economic growth as part of the Russian Presidency's focus on growth. The Issues Paper, prepared by OECD, analyzes the channels through which corruption affects economic performance and the complex factors hampering the economic potential of countries affected by corruption.

Supporting Domestic Law Enforcement Efforts in Pursuing Cases

To complement incentives from other government departments, development agencies may consider allocating development assistance funds to support domestic law enforcement units dedicated to investigating and prosecuting corruption cases that may secure the return of illegally acquired assets to developing countries. Experience in the United Kingdom demonstrates that results can be achieved in terms of cases and dollars frozen or returned (Mason 2013, 198; see also box 8.1). If a country undertakes such efforts, continuity of personnel and resources is very important, as the relationships will bear fruit only if sustained over some time.

Advising on Ways to Secure Asset Return

UNCAC provides a framework for the return of the proceeds of corruption to the country of origin or to the direct victims of the individual offenses (or both). On occasion, courts have ordered compensation "for the benefit of the people" of the country of the corrupt official. In such cases, development agencies have participated by advising the domestic

---

BOX 8.1	Good Practice: Development Agencies Finance Law Enforcement Efforts to Combat Corruption and Recover Assets

Since 2006 the U.K. Department for International Development (DFID) has funded the Proceeds of Corruption Unit (POCU) in the Metropolitan Police. POCU employs 11 officers who specialize in cases involving the alleged laundering of corrupt assets in the United Kingdom. DFID also funds the City of London Police Overseas Anti-Corruption Unit (OACU), with 12 specialist officers who investigate allegations of corruption in developing countries that involve U.K. citizens, companies, or financial institutions. And it supports dedicated posts for developing-country cases within the Crown Prosecution Service, which is responsible for executing confiscation orders.

Over six years of operation, the POCU cost DFID £5 million, or about $8.14 million, in total. The units have been actively involved in investigations in close collaboration with Arab Republic of Egypt, Malawi, Nigeria, Uganda, and Zambia. They have pursued prosecutions through the U.K. courts, provided evidence for prosecutions overseas, and supported the freezing and confiscation of assets, including securing the conviction in a U.K. court of the former Nigerian state governor James Ibori, several of his associates, and his U.K. solicitor.

DFID's return on investment continues to be good, with more than £100 million in frozen assets currently subject to judicial procedures with a view to confiscation (Mason 2013, 203).

In December 2010, BAE Systems settled allegations of bribery with the United Kingdom. In a plea agreement, the company agreed to pay reparations of £30 million. The court's only stipulation was that the payment should be "for the benefit of the people of Tanzania in a manner to be agreed upon between the Serious Fraud Office (SFO) and BAE."[a]

The U.K. Department for International Development (DFID) initially became involved in providing advice to the Serious Fraud Office during the plea agreement process, based on discussions with the government of Tanzania regarding best options for use of the funds (activities should support the Tanzanian government's development strategy), potential problems, and specific areas where DFID could offer technical advice.

Following an agreement that the government of Tanzania would develop a proposal for use of the funds, DFID offered guidance to the SFO and the government of Tanzania in the preparation of the proposal. That included advice on ring-fencing the payment for specific development objectives, setting up measurable development objectives, monitoring and evaluation, and drafting a good quality proposal.

In November 2010 the government of Tanzania formally proposed to the SFO to use the money to buy essential teaching materials and to improve classroom facilities and teacher accommodations. The proposal outlined how the money would be disbursed, with the process monitored and subject to an independent evaluation and audit. The proposal was accepted by the SFO, and BAE agreed to it in 2011.

DFID continues to help the government of Tanzania monitor the expenditure of these funds. Although there have been some difficulties, the upside is that no corruption-related problems have arisen from the disbursement.

a. Settlement Agreement between the SFO and BAE Systems Plc, February 2010. The company also pleaded guilty to one count of record-keeping violations under Section 221 of the Companies Act 1985 and was sentenced to pay a fine of £500,000 (which was deducted from the ex-gratia payment) and £225,000 for prosecution costs. As a result, no corruption charges were brought by the U.K. Serious Fraud Office.

agency responsible for the asset return and collaborating with the foreign authorities to develop the framework and mechanism for giving effect to the returns. Box 8.2 provides an example of how the U.K. DFID worked with the U.K. Serious Fraud Office and the government of Tanzania on a proposal for the use of reparations that the court ordered should be "for the benefit of the people of Tanzania."

Adequate Financing for Capacity-Building Efforts in Developing Countries

Improving the capacity of countries is a major tenet of the Accra Agenda for Action and the aid effectiveness forum in general. In the context of asset recovery, developing-country practitioners are often in need of technical assistance to support effective domestic investigations, including gathering evidence, tracing assets, and working with foreign jurisdictions. Development agencies can fund programs or activities such as the ones described below, to build capacity to conduct effective investigations:

- International and bilateral meetings of practitioners for case discussions, strategic discussions, and sharing of good practices
- Mentorship and training programs for foreign law enforcement agencies, including exchanges and secondments of law enforcement officials
- Placement of liaison magistrates, officers, and police attachés in other regions or jurisdictions
- Technical assistance that builds the capacity of foreign law enforcement officials to cooperate on international cases
- Meetings of practitioner networks, including global or regional asset recovery networks (for example, the Global Focal Point Network of StAR/Interpol, CARIN, ARINSA, ARIN-EA, ARIN-AP, RRAG) or law enforcement cooperation such as Interpol.

Facilitating Data Collection

In many countries, the data on asset recovery are held by several different agencies and by both federal and state or provincial actors. Development agencies could facilitate coordinating the collection and aggregation of nonsensitive data currently dispersed across multiple agencies or at different government levels.

Communicating Asset Recovery Policies, Actions, and Results

Development agencies can communicate the importance of asset recovery, sharing successful developments and achievements and encouraging the gathering of statistics to show results. These messages are important both domestically and for developing countries and will support both asset recovery efforts and the transparency and accountability goals of the Accra Agenda for Action. For example, in the United Kingdom, DFID provides the secretariat function for a cross-government politically exposed persons (PEPs) strategic group that brings together the main agencies with interests in international PEP issues, such as the national treasury, the financial regulator, investigative and prosecution agencies, and ministries for business, justice, and foreign affairs (Mason 2013, 202).

Advocating Policies, Laws, and Institutional Development

Development agencies can use their position and financing to advocate for the policies, laws, and institutional developments that this report recommends, both at home and abroad. They can also support the efforts of civil society organizations and the media in knowledge development and sharing and advocacy.

Ultimately it is important to recognize that progress will take place over the long term, as institutional capacity is built, legal and investigative tools are put in place, and cases are conducted. Actual cases will be time-consuming, complex, and expensive. Development agencies are well placed to give support through policy and legal advice, knowledge generation, capacity building, and funding. And they must do so if they are to meet their commitments in the Accra Agenda for Action and Busan partnership.

Recommendation:

Development agencies need to expand their efforts in fighting corruption and recovering assets. In addition to the technical assistance that can be provided to foreign countries are possible actions at the domestic level:

- Incorporate anticorruption and asset recovery efforts into development policies.
- Support domestic law enforcement's pursuit of cases.
- Ensure adequate financing for prevention and capacity building in developing countries.
- Facilitate data collection.
- Communicate asset recovery policies, actions, and results.
- Advocate for pertinent policies, laws, and institutional development.

References

Mason, P. 2013. "Being Janus: A Donor Agency's Approach to Asset Recovery." In *Emerging Trends in Asset Recovery,* edited by G. F. Zinkemagel, C. Monteith, and P. Gomes Pereira. Bern: Peter Lang AG, International Academic Publishers.

G20 Anticorruption Working Group. 2013. "Issues Paper on Corruption and Economic Growth." St. Petersburg, Russia. Available at http://www.oecd.org/g20/topics/anti-corruption/Issue-Paper-Corruption-and-Economic-Growth.pdf.

9. Conclusions

Few and Far: Despite some efforts to advance the asset recovery agenda in a handful of countries, relatively few assets are being recovered and the amounts are far from the billions of dollars that are estimated stolen from developing countries each year. Most OECD countries reported little progress, and fourteen of the 34 OECD members did not responding at all. There is much room for improvement and to make significant advancements in the asset recovery agenda.

This report outlines some of the positive trends or results in asset recovery between 2010 and June 2012, including:

- **The use of administrative actions to freeze assets.** The introduction of administrative freezes in the context of the Arab Spring helped countries to rapidly freeze assets and resulted in an increased level of assets frozen.
- **Proactive actions by developed countries.** More jurisdictions are proactively initiating their own domestic investigations, rather than waiting for a request from the jurisdiction of the corrupt official.
- **The expansion of the toolkit beyond criminal confiscation.** The use of non-conviction based asset confiscation, court-ordered reparations and restitution, and settlement agreements were used to return more assets than was criminal confiscation–commonly thought to be the main legal avenue for asset recovery.
- **A higher proportion of assets being returned to developing countries.**
- **Successful recovery is achieved in countries with established policies, solid laws and organizational structures, and a willingness to try alternatives in the face of barriers.**

Success in stolen asset recovery requires action by all stakeholders involved, including law enforcement and justice officials, requesting and requested jurisdictions, banks, private companies and their intermediaries (such as lawyers), development agencies, civil society, and the media.

Development agencies have committed themselves to recover the proceeds of corruption in the Agenda in the Accra Agenda for Action and the Busan Partnership. This report has explored the various actions that development agencies can take, whether in prevention, advocacy, policy development, facilitating data collection, communicating policies and results, funding technical assistance programs or domestic law enforcement, and advising on modalities for asset return (where requested). Through these activities, development agencies will support the main recommendations of the report outlined below.

1. Obtain a high-level commitment to asset recovery.
2. Provide the necessary resources, whether for investigations, international cooperation, policy development work, preventive measures, or technical assistance programs.
3. Ensure that a wide range of asset recovery tools are available and used.
4. Be proactive, not reactive.
5. Build capacity in developing countries.
6. Collect statistics to measure results, and make them publicly available.

Appendix A. Recommendations

Main Recommendations from the Executive Summary

1. *Obtain a high-level commitment to asset recovery.* Both developed and developing countries need to adopt and implement comprehensive strategic policies to combat corruption and recover assets. For their part, development agencies need establish asset recovery as a priority in their strategic planning.
2. *Provide necessary resources.* Adequate funding is needed to support asset recovery, including funding for investigations, prosecutions, international cooperation, training of domestic and foreign practitioners, policy development work, and institutions. Development agencies can allocate development funds to support these programs, both domestically and in foreign jurisdictions.
3. *Ensure that a wide range of asset recovery tools are available and used.* Both developed and developing countries need to ensure that they have a broad range of mechanisms in place, such as the ability to rapidly freeze assets, to confiscate in the absence of a conviction, to return assets as part of a settlement agreement, and to reverse or shift the burden of proof.
4. *Be proactive, not reactive.* OECD members need to ensure they are able to proactively identify and freeze assets of allegedly corrupt officials and should establish incentives for domestic practitioners to initiate cases. Such domestic actions should be followed by international cooperation with the relevant foreign jurisdiction, including the use of spontaneous disclosures and actions to build capacity and trust. Developing countries need to be initiating their own investigations and communicating and cooperating with foreign counterparts.
5. *Build capacity in developing countries.* Asset recovery requires effective investigations in both the requested and requesting countries, and many developing countries may need technical assistance to take action. Development agencies can support the training and mentoring of developing-country practitioners, especially given that capacity development is a priority of the Accra Agenda and is key to achieving development results.
6. *Collect statistics to measure results and make them publicly available.* Statistics on law enforcement efforts are essential for showing that countries are fulfilling their high-level commitments; they also help to guide domestic policy development, resource allocation, and strategic planning. Making progress publicly available highlights these results and also supports transparency and accountability—the essential elements for development results outlined in the Accra Agenda.

Additional Recommendations

The following are the recommendations listed throughout the report. They are meant to complement the main recommendations with additional clarification and specific actions for key stakeholders.

Data Collection (from chapter 2)

Developed and developing countries should maintain comprehensive statistics on asset recovery cases, including assets frozen and confiscated, reparations or restitution ordered, and assets returned. Gaps in the data should be identified and their collection addressed. Where possible, countries should gather data on the various means to return assets, including criminal and non-conviction based (NCB) confiscation, administrative confiscation, private civil actions, and other forms of direct recovery. Statistics on cases and information on laws and results should be publicly available and accessible in a central location such as a website.

Policy Recommendations (from chapter 4)

Developed and developing countries should adopt, implement, and fund comprehensive strategic policies to combat corruption and recover assets. Countries should identify gaps and be swift and responsive in addressing obstacles encountered during the asset recovery process. They should evaluate the implementation of these policies and consider changes where needed.

Legal Recommendations (from chapter 5)

Germany, Japan, and New Zealand should ratify the UNCAC.

To be effective in asset recovery, OECD member states should develop laws and regulations to adequate for accomplishing the following:

- Rapidly freeze assets prior to an MLA request.
- Confiscate assets in the absence of a conviction (e.g., NCB confiscation).
- Permit direct enforcement of foreign criminal or NCB orders and international cooperation based on NCB cases.
- Require that service providers collect beneficial ownership information and allow access to it.
- Permit spontaneous disclosures and other means to share information on the freeze with the foreign jurisdiction.
- Help practitioners overcome barriers in asset recovery, (for example, laws introducing legal presumptions, unexplained wealth or illicit enrichment provisions, extended confiscation, confiscation of equivalent value).

Countries should engage in a domestic or international policy debate on how asset returns can be incorporated into settlement agreements in corruption cases.

They should consider necessary legislative changes to permit the inclusion of third parties in settlement agreements in foreign bribery cases.

Operational Recommendations (from chapter 6)

The following steps are recommended for OECD members:

- Establish and adequately resource specialized teams or units to work on asset recovery cases. Such teams must be staffed with personnel who are specialized in asset recovery cases and have expertise in financial investigation and forensic accounting and with attorneys who have experience in asset recovery.
- Establish incentives for domestic law enforcement to proactively initiate domestic cases of money laundering or foreign bribery.
- Engage in and use practitioner networks.
- Conduct capacity-building efforts in developing countries to support effective investigations, international cooperation, and the sharing of good practices.

Recommendations for Developing Countries (from chapter 7)

Developing countries should increase their efforts to combat corruption and recover assets, including the following steps:

- Obtain high-level political commitment to asset recovery, as well as the commitment and involvement of the various domestic stakeholders.
- Adopt and implement necessary legislative and institutional changes, in particular NCB confiscation and mechanisms to rapidly freeze assets.
- Conduct cases and investigations.
- Engage in international cooperation using both informal practitioner-to-practitioner channels and formal mutual legal assistance.
- Develop domestic capacity to conduct cases, reaching out to development agencies and international organizations where required.

Recommendations for Development Agencies (from chapter 8)

Development agencies need to expand their efforts in fighting corruption and recovering assets. In addition to the technical assistance that can be provided to foreign countries, possible actions at the domestic level include the following:

- Incorporate anticorruption and asset recovery efforts into development policies.
- Support domestic law enforcement efforts in pursuing cases.
- Ensure adequate financing for prevention and capacity building in developing countries.
- Facilitate data collection.
- Communicate asset recovery policies, actions, and results.
- Advocate for pertinent policies, laws, and institutional development.

Appendix B. Nine Key Principles of Effective Asset Recovery Adopted by the G20 Anticorruption Working Group, Cannes, 2011

Policy Development

1. **Make asset recovery a policy priority; align resources to support policy.** To make progress on domestic commitments and international cooperation, such a policy could help communicate the importance of asset recovery as an integral part of broader anti-corruption efforts, empower authorities leading asset recovery cases, mobilize them with the appropriate resources and expertise to trace, seize and confiscate stolen assets, promote the proactive pursuit of cases (rather than waiting for an MLA request), and encourage the widest range of assistance to other countries. It would identify the steps needed to promote, sustain, and strengthen the development of specialized expertise in the appropriate bodies and include a legislative agenda for addressing any gaps in existing laws or for adopting any other measures to support implementation of the policy. The policy would serve to define goals and targets and to make stakeholders accountable.

Legislative Framework

2. **Strengthen preventive measures against the proceeds of corruption.** Strengthened preventive mechanisms to protect the financial system against the proceeds of corruption are critical. Measures requiring that financial institutions and designated non financial businesses and professions (DNFBPs) conduct customer due diligence, identify and monitor PEPs, and collect and make available beneficial ownership information are essential in this regard: without obtaining this information, subsequent asset tracing, freezing, and confiscation efforts are rendered futile. It is also essential that supervisory authorities effectively enforce these requirements, and make public such enforcement actions.

3. **Set up tools for rapid locating and freezing of assets.** To facilitate the prompt identification of bank assets that may be proceeds of corruption, establishing tools that would allow competent authorities to obtain information from financial institutions in a timely fashion to determine whether an individual has access to banking facilities in that jurisdiction is critical. Such a search could be initiated upon appropriate domestic or international request. This could be achieved either through a central register of bank accounts that can be accessed by competent

authorities or through a system which allows competent authorities to direct query all banks within a jurisdiction. The system should also enable competent authorities to rapidly freeze assets, whether through a temporary administrative freeze, automatic freeze upon the filing of charges or an arrest, or by order of an investigating magistrate or prosecutor.

4. **Establish a wide range of options for asset recovery, such as non-conviction based proceedings and private law actions.** While a *criminal prosecution* is a common component of a corruption case, past cases demonstrate that *criminal confiscation* is not always appropriate to recover the proceeds of corruption (see Asset Recovery Database Factsheet). It is essential to ensure that there are multiple avenues for asset recovery, in particular systems that allow for recovery through non-conviction based confiscation (at a minimum in cases of death, flight, absence), unexplained wealth orders, and private (civil) law actions. Further, consistent with the UNCAC, it is necessary to have in place the legal and institutional framework to allow for direct recovery and the return of confiscated proceeds of corruption to prior legitimate owners, subject to the rights of bona fide third parties.

5. **Adopt laws that encourage and facilitate international cooperation.** Laws that permit foreign authorities to obtain all relevant information on the proceeds of corruption in a timely manner and to enable prompt legal action in response to foreign requests are the cornerstone of asset recovery efforts. They should

    a. Permit the direct enforcement of foreign orders, including non-conviction based confiscation orders. Such orders should be permitted even in the absence of a domestic system for non-conviction based confiscation or other avenue.

    b. Ensure that mutual legal assistance be granted in the absence of a bilateral legal assistance agreement (i.e., an ad hoc basis) when dealing with asset recovery of PEPs. In addition, laws should permit UNCAC as a sufficient legal basis for mutual legal assistance.

    c. Ensure that MLA requests for freezing be permitted on an ex parte basis (i.e., no requirement to give the asset holder the opportunity to contest the provision of MLA).

Institutional Framework

6. **Create specialized asset recovery teams—a kleptocracy unit.** Success is closely related to the existence of specialized team of investigators and prosecutors that focus on the recovery of assets, including on behalf of countries harmed by grand corruption (in some jurisdictions, an asset recovery office may fill this role). Such units should be properly resourced, have proper expertise and training, and have access to relevant databases, registries, and financial information to allow practitioners to identify, locate, and freeze assets. They should also have authority to cooperate with foreign FIUs, law enforcement, and judicial authorities, and to provide technical assistance in "following the money" to third party countries.

7. **Actively participate into international cooperation networks.** National institutional frameworks should be set up to ensure that foreign authorities are able to

obtain all relevant information on the proceeds of corruption in a timely manner and to enable prompt legal action in response to foreign requests. Such institutional frameworks include

a. **Establishing focal points of contact** for law enforcement and clear and effective channels for mutual legal assistance requests related to corruption and asset recovery.

b. **Working with existing networks (policy or operational),** such as UNCAC, Interpol/StAR, the International Corruption Hunters Alliance, CARIN, and the meeting of law enforcement authorities at the OECD, amongst others to identify possible gaps and identify best course of action in multi-countries international investigations and prosecutions.

c. **Encourage informal contacts with foreign counterparts** particularly before the presentation of mutual legal assistance requests.

d. **Make information publicly available** on what assistance does or does not require an official MLA request and applicable procedures and legal requirements for pre-MLA and MLA international cooperation (including whether UNCAC is a sufficient basis for MLA).

e. **Encourage spontaneous disclosures by domestic authorities,** a proactive form of assistance which alerts a foreign jurisdiction to an ongoing investigation in the disclosing jurisdiction and indicates that existing evidence could be of interest.

f. **Improve capacity to respond to MLA requests in grand corruption cases.** Granting mutual legal assistance even in cases of minor technical or formal deficiencies should be the norm. Allocating increased staff and resources to work with the foreign jurisdiction in the drafting or clarification of requests will help to avoid such deficiencies.

8. **Provide technical assistance to developing countries.** Past cases demonstrate that asset recovery and international cooperation usually require a domestic criminal investigation and proceedings in the jurisdiction harmed by corruption. To build up sufficient expertise in all countries, developed jurisdictions should provide technical assistance on how to investigate, restrain and confiscate the proceeds of corruption to those countries in need of it. Training or mentorship programs that enable the achievement of results in cases over the long-term should be the primary focus in this regard; and assistance should be coordinated among the donors. Other jurisdictions which lack such expertise should undertake to request such assistance from donors and international organizations.

9. **Collect data on cases and share information on impact and results.** To ensure the momentum for action is maintained, it is very important to step up the tracking of measures and operational actions being taken. It is also very important to track actual asset recovery cases, to show that "it works". Existing forums, such as the UNCAC Asset Recovery Working Group, the OECD anti-bribery working group or CARIN and similar networks, should be used for discussions of asset recovery cases (even if only when completed) and exchanges on lessons learned. Where information on cases is public, countries should ensure that this information is shared more broadly, such as by providing the case details for inclusion in the StAR Asset Recovery Database.

Appendix C. StAR/OECD Questionnaire

This questionnaire is developed by the World Bank/Stolen Asset Recovery Initiative (StAR) and OECD Development Assistance Committee as a means to collect data for a follow-up assessment[1] on the progress that member countries have made in meeting their Accra/Busan commitments[2] to combat corruption and to track, freeze, and recover illegally acquired assets. These questions aim to gather data on international asset recovery[3] efforts in corruption cases,[4] including money-laundering cases where corruption is a predicate offense. To facilitate your efforts, section D of the questionnaire has been pre populated with data from the StAR Asset Recovery Watch[5] and the StAR Settlement Databases.[6] Please elaborate answers as needed, and your efforts to include additional documents or brochures describing programs, policies, or initiatives would be greatly appreciated.

A. General Information

Country:	
Name of reporting agency:	
Contact name and email for follow up:	
Currency used:	

---

1. For first assessment from 2006 to 2009, see "Tracking Anti-Corruption and Asset Recovery Commitments: A Progress Report and Recommendations for Action" (StAR/OECD DAC, November 2011).

2. Accra Agenda for Action (adopted at the Third High Level Forum on Aid Effectiveness) para 24: and the Busan Partnership for Effective Development Cooperation (adopted at the Fourth High Level Forum on Aid Effectiveness) para 33.

3. International asset recovery is defined as the process of tracing, freezing, and returning illegally acquired assets to a foreign jurisdiction.

4. Corruption is defined as those offenses listed in the United Nations Convention Against Corruption, Articles 15–23, namely bribery of national public officials; bribery of foreign officials and officials of public international organizations; embezzlement, misappropriation or other diversion of property by a public official; trading in influence; abuse of functions; illicit enrichment; bribery in the private sector; embezzlement of property in the private sector; and laundering of proceeds of crime. It includes money-laundering cases where corruption is a predicate offence.

5. StAR Asset Recovery Watch is a joint UNODC and World Bank project, systematically compiling information on completed and active recovery cases involving corruption. The database can be found at: http://www1.worldbank.org/finance/star_site/star-watch.html.

6. Settlement Database" - StAR Database of Settlements of Foreign Bribery and Related Cases, a comprehensive database of completed settlement cases of foreign bribery and related cases, will be available on the website of the Stolen Asset Recovery Network Initiative in late 2012. Database will be open for public viewing and use.

B. Policy and Legislative Framework

1.	Between 2010- June 2012, has your jurisdiction adopted any new policies aimed at enhancing and facilitating international asset recovery? (please provide the name of the policy)		
2.	Between 2010- June 2012, has your jurisdiction adopted any new laws and/or regulations aimed at enhancing and facilitating international asset recovery? (If yes, please provide the name(s) of the law(s))		
3.	Does your jurisdiction permit the rapid[7] freezing of assets of corrupt foreign officials based on a request from a foreign jurisdiction? How does a rapid freezing request get approved?	Y	N
4.	Does your jurisdiction permit direct enforcement of foreign confiscation orders?	Y	N
5.	Does your jurisdiction allow non-conviction based (NCB) asset confiscation?	Y	N
6.	Does your jurisdiction recognize foreign NCB orders?	Y	N
7.	Do you allow foreign countries to initiate civil actions in your domestic courts to recover proceeds?	Y	N
8.	Do you permit courts (or other competent authorities) to order compensation, restitution, or other damages to the benefit of a foreign jurisdiction? Describe the relevant legal frameworks, and any limitations: _____	Y	N

C. Institutional Framework

1.	Does your jurisdiction have a specialized prosecution and/or investigative unit focused on pursuing corruption and international asset recovery cases? (please provide the name)
2.	What types of resources has your jurisdiction allocated over the past two years to enhance the fight against foreign corruption (including corruption-related money laundering) and/or to facilitate international asset recovery in corruption cases? <table><tr><td>Training</td><td>Staffing</td><td>Funding</td><td>Other</td></tr></table>
3.	Please list any programs/projects in place to support developing countries in strengthening their capacity to investigate and prosecute corruption cases and return stolen assets (e.g., MLA support, mentorships, study-tours, funding for domestic law enforcement units, etc).

D. Summary of International Asset Recovery Efforts in Corruption Cases

1. **Summary Table:** To the extent possible, please report on international asset recovery efforts in corruption cases between 2010 and June 2012 (either initiated or completed cases).

---

7. "Rapid" is defined as a period between 24 and 48 hours.

		Assets Identified	Assets Frozen	Assets Confiscated	Assets Returned
1.	No. of Cases				
2.	Total Value				

2. **<u>Asset Freezing Orders:</u>** Please list up to 10 of your largest international asset recovery cases involving corruption where money or assets have been **<u>frozen</u>** between 2010 and June 2012. If you only have available data until end 2011 then please make a note of this in the responses.

*To facilitate your efforts, this section of the questionnaire has been pre populated with data from the StAR Asset Recovery Watch – but **we ask that you please review and revise this data**.*

No.	Amount	Originating Country	How was Case Initiated? (Check All that Apply)
1.			☐ MLA ☐ Domestic investigation ☐ Other _____
2.			☐ MLA ☐ Domestic investigation ☐ Other _____
3.			☐ MLA ☐ Domestic investigation ☐ Other _____
4.			☐ MLA ☐ Domestic investigation ☐ Other _____
5.			☐ MLA ☐ Domestic investigation ☐ Other _____
6.			☐ MLA ☐ Domestic investigation ☐ Other _____
7.			☐ MLA ☐ Domestic investigation ☐ Other _____
8.			☐ MLA ☐ Domestic investigation ☐ Other _____

(continued next page)

No.	Amount	Originating Country	How was Case Initiated? (Check All that Apply)
9.			☐ MLA ☐ Domestic investigation ☐ Other _____
10.			☐ MLA ☐ Domestic investigation ☐ Other _____

3. **Assets Returned:** Please list up to 10 of your largest international asset recovery cases involving corruption where money or assets have been **returned** between 2010 and June 2012.

*To facilitate your efforts, this section of the questionnaire has been pre populated with data from the StAR Asset Recovery Watch – but **we ask that you please review and revise this data**.*

No.	Amount	Originating Country	How was Case Initiated? (Check All that Apply)
1.			☐ MLA ☐ Domestic investigation ☐ Other _____
2.			☐ MLA ☐ Domestic investigation ☐ Other _____
3.			☐ MLA ☐ Domestic investigation ☐ Other _____
4.			☐ MLA ☐ Domestic investigation ☐ Other _____
5.			☐ MLA ☐ Domestic investigation ☐ Other _____
6.			☐ MLA ☐ Domestic investigation ☐ Other _____
7.			☐ MLA ☐ Domestic investigation ☐ Other _____

(continued next page)

No.	Amount	Originating Country	How was Case Initiated? (Check All that Apply)
8.			☐ MLA ☐ Domestic investigation ☐ Other _____
9.			☐ MLA ☐ Domestic investigation ☐ Other _____
10.			☐ MLA ☐ Domestic investigation ☐ Other _____

4. **<u>Payment of Compensation or Damages in criminal cases:</u>** Some states have chosen to award compensation or damages to foreign jurisdictions, an option provided for in UNCAC article 53 b. The following table aims to capture cases in which this option has been used.

Please list corruption cases that have resulted in orders of compensation or restitution to a foreign jurisdiction between 2010 and June 2012. This should include returns pursuant to a settlement agreement.

No.	Amount	Originating Country	How was Case Initiated? (Check All that Apply)
1.			☐ MLA ☐ Domestic investigation ☐ Other _____
2.			☐ MLA ☐ Domestic investigation ☐ Other _____
3.			☐ MLA ☐ Domestic investigation ☐ Other _____
4.			☐ MLA ☐ Domestic investigation ☐ Other _____
5.			☐ MLA ☐ Domestic investigation ☐ Other _____

5. **Other mechanisms used for asset return:** Please list cases in which the asset return to a foreign jurisdiction has been accomplished through another mechanism not indicated above, as well as mechanism used, such as for example:
- Direct recoveries/returns resulting from private civil actions by foreign governments (UNCAC Art 53 a),
- Funds/assets provided to a third-party or charitable organization to be used for activities in the originating country

No.	Originating Country	Assets Returned	Mechanisms Used
1.			
2.			
3.			
4.			

6. **Other:** Please feel free to provide any other relevant data or information.

E. Data Collection

1.	Is there a system in place for the systematic collection of data on international asset recovery cases?	Y	N
2.	Identify all the difficulties encountered in data collection, check all that apply: _____ Data collected at federal level but not at state/provincial level _____ Data on domestic and foreign cases is not counted separately _____ Data on money laundering cases does not distinguish the predicate offense of corruption _____ Domestic coordination _____ Information is sensitive and cannot be shared Other _____		

www.ingramcontent.com/pod-product-compliance
Lightning Source LLC
Chambersburg PA
CBHW081646280326
41928CB00069B/3126